BLUEPHIES

NEW AMERICAN
COOKING

BLUEPHIES

NEW AMERICAN
COOKING

Recipes your
Mom never
made you

Bill Horzuesky

ITCHY CAT PRESS • BLUE MOUNDS, WISCONSIN

First edition, first printing, 2005
Text copyright © 2005 Bill Horzuesky

Itchy Cat Press
A Division of Flying Fish Graphics
5452 Highway K
Blue Mounds, Wisconsin 53517
ffg@mhtc.net

Designed and produced by
Flying Fish Graphics
Blue Mounds, Wisconsin

Photographs © 2005 Brent Nicastro
Other photos pages 2 & 13, by Joey Connaughty
photos pages 37 & 57, by Caroline Beckett
Printed in Korea

Library of Congress Control Number: 2005931624

ISBN 0-9761450-1-4

Itchy
Cat
Press

Contents

Here go the thanks

A special thanks to the people who made this book and the restaurant possible. First and foremost, Melanie—my wife and best friend—thanks for being a believer. Your continual support makes it possible for me to do what I love. You are the best.

Thanks to Food Fight for the opportunity to do this project. I think we truly made a cool restaurant and a timeless book. Handshakes for some and hugs for others. You know who you are. Thanks for all your help, Joey.

Frank and Caroline from Itchy Cat, thanks for being there to help put my life on paper. "I'll know it when I see it" finally got accomplished.

Brent, thanks for capturing the nuts and bolts of this place. I wanted to show people what a working restaurant was all about, and you got it.

Thanks to my three boys who are always happy to see me no matter what time I get home.

Last but not least, thanks to the entire staff at the restaurant. You are the ones who get the job done every day and I really appreciate that.

Thanks and good luck to all of you.

SOUPS

Soup Tips from the Chef

Make your own soup stock. It will take more time, but will make valuable use of vegetable scraps and meat trimmings. You can also use pre-made broth, found in any grocery store. If you use soup base, add water to equal the amount of stock required.

I tend to use vegetable stock for my soups because of its neutral flavor—and we have a lot of vegetable trimmings at the restaurant. Peppers, eggplant and cabbage DO NOT belong in a stockpot because their flavors get too strong and overpower the broth.

When cutting vegetables for the soups, make the pieces equal size to ensure even cooking. However, if you are planning to purée the soup, just rough-chop the vegetables to save yourself some time.

I recommend cooling soup BEFORE you purée it. Hot soup causes nasty burns, which I promise will last longer than your soup.

You can use fresh herbs in place of dried herbs in a stock, but remember that fresh is always less potent than dried. If you use fresh herbs, use 1/3 the amount as dried, so 1 tablespoon fresh = 1 teaspoon dried, in most cases.

Use garnishes—they can make the soup a meal. Fried thin slices of vegetables, julienned fresh herbs, crisp tortillas, sour cream, or chile purées work well. The more creative you get, the better your soup will be.

The soups in this cookbook, with the exception of Gazpacho, freeze pretty well. But remember that freezing soups will alter some of their main characteristics such as consistency, flavor and texture.

Billy's Five-Spice Black Bean Soup *(next page) garnished with sour cream, cilantro, and* Pickled Corn Relish *(page 59)*

Billy's Five-Spice Black Bean Soup

1/4 cup vegetable or olive oil
1 carrot, chopped
2 stalks celery, chopped
1/2 yellow large onion, chopped
1 tablespoon minced fresh garlic
1 teaspoon dried ginger
1 tablespoon Chinese Five-Spice Blend (page 55)
1/2 tablespoon dried curry powder
2 tablespoons soup base (vegetable or chicken)
1 cup canned puréed tomatoes
2 tablespoons soy sauce
1 pound dried black beans
3 quarts water
Salt and pepper

Do not soak the beans overnight. They will cook to the correct texture if you just sort, rinse, and toss them in the pot.

Heat vegetable or olive oil in a 2- to 3-gallon stockpot. Add carrots, celery, onion, and garlic and sauté, stirring occasionally, until all vegetables are softened, about 10 minutes.

Stir ginger, Chinese five-spice, curry, and soup base into the vegetables. Sauté for an additional 5 minutes. Stir in tomatoes, soy sauce, black beans, and water. Simmer the soup, stirring occasionally, until the black beans are very tender, 1–1/2 to 2 hours. Season with salt and pepper to taste.

Serving options

1. If you prefer a puréed black bean soup, let the soup cool to lukewarm. Purée in batches in a blender until all the soup is puréed. Reheat and serve with a scoop of sour cream on top.

2. If you prefer the beans and vegetables whole, be sure to chop the vegetables uniformly when preparing them for the soup. I suggest that you chop all vegetables about 1/4 inch square.

Makes 2–3 quarts.

Butternut Squash Soup

I make so much of this soup during the fall and winter that it's exhausting. Just when I think there is a slight warming trend and I can retire the squash soup for the year—KA-BLAM! COLD SNAP! Then I am right back in the kitchen, roasting the squash for the next ten-gallon batch.

2 tablespoons olive oil
4 celery stalks, chopped
1 large yellow onion, chopped
1 tablespoon minced fresh garlic
1/2 cup brown sugar
1 tablespoon dried thyme
1 teaspoon dried oregano
1 teaspoon Chinese Five-Spice Blend (page 55)
2 tablespoons curry powder
1 tablespoon dried ginger
2 tablespoons soup base (vegetable or chicken)
5 roasted butternut squash, skins and seeds removed (next page)
1 cup fresh or canned puréed tomatoes
10 cups water
2 cups heavy cream
Salt and pepper

Heat oil in a large saucepan over medium heat. Add celery and onion and sauté, stirring occasionally, until the onion turns a light brown. Add the garlic and sauté for about 2 more minutes. Add the sugar, thyme, oregano, five-spice, curry, ginger, and soup base. Sauté until fragrant, 2–3 minutes.

Add the roasted squash flesh at this point. Add the tomatoes, water, and cream. Sit back and let it simmer into soup—until it reduces by about a quarter. Purée until smooth with a hand-held blender directly in the saucepan (or in batches in a food processor). Add salt and pepper to taste if needed.

Note: Okay—here is the cool part: If you want more of an Asian influence, use 1 tablespoon of sesame oil instead of the olive oil and add more five-spice. Lemongrass is great, too. Or spice it up with some chipotle. You get the idea—mix it up.

Makes 10 or more servings.

How to Roast Winter Squash for Soups

Wash and dry the squash. Trim a small slice off the bottom to make a flat surface. Place flat side down on a cutting board. Cut the squash in half through the top.

Place the halves cut side down in a shallow baking dish. Add water to 1/4 inch level. Cover with aluminum foil. Bake at 350 degrees until tender, about 45 minutes to 1 hour.

Remove the squash from the pan and let it cool slightly. Scoop the seeds out and discard them. Scoop the squash out and use it in soup. You can save the shell and use it for a serving dish if you like.

Another Way to Roast Winter Squash

Cut the top of the squash off and discard it. Cut the squash in half through the width. Scrape out the seeds and membranes with a sturdy spoon. Coat the squash halves, inside and out, with olive or vegetable oil.

Place the halves on a cookie sheet, cut side down. (If you line the pan with parchment paper first, clean up will be easy.) Roast in a 350-degree oven for about an hour. It's done when the squash is soft, and the flesh has caramelized a little (which makes it sweeter).

Gazpacho

1 can (about 16 ounces) puréed tomatoes
1/2 cup extra-virgin olive oil
2 teaspoons minced fresh garlic
1/8 cup whole fresh cilantro leaves
5 dashes Tabasco
1 tablespoon lemon juice
3 cups soup broth (vegetable, chicken or beef)
1 medium cucumber, peeled, seeded and chopped
1/2 medium red onion, finely diced
1/2 poblano pepper, finely diced
1/2 red pepper, finely diced
Salt and pepper
Sour cream
Fried tortilla strips* (use store-bought)

Combine the tomatoes, olive oil, garlic, cilantro, Tabasco, lemon juice, and soup broth in a large bowl. Purée it with a hand blender (or in a food processor).

Add the chopped cucumbers, onion, poblano pepper, and red pepper. Mix well; cover the bowl and place in the refrigerator overnight to let the flavors blend. Season to taste with salt and pepper.

Serve chilled and garnish each serving with sour cream and fried tortilla strips.

Makes 4–6 servings.

*Cut tortillas in 1/2 inch strips. Fry in oil heated to 350 degrees until crisp.

Lentil Soup

1/4 cup vegetable or olive oil
1 carrot, diced
2 stalks celery, diced
1/2 large yellow onion, diced
1 tablespoon minced fresh garlic
2 cups chopped cooked turkey, ham or chicken (optional)
2 tablespoons soup base (vegetable or chicken)
1 tablespoon dried thyme
2 teaspoons dried oregano
1/2 teaspoon dried rosemary
1 1/2 pounds lentils (green, red, brown or yellow)
2 cups canned puréed tomatoes
1 gallon water
2 1/2 tablespoons salt
1 tablespoon black pepper

Heat the oil in a 2- to 3-gallon stockpot over medium heat. Sauté the carrots until they have started to soften, about 5 minutes. Add celery to the carrots and cook until they have softened, about 3 minutes more. Add the onion and garlic; sauté until the onion is translucent.

If you are using meat in this recipe, add it at this point, so that it will blend well with the soup. For a vegetarian version, skip the meat.

Add the vegetable or chicken soup base, thyme, oregano, rosemary, lentils, tomatoes, water, salt, and pepper to the stockpot. Simmer on medium-low heat, stirring every so often, until the lentils are tender, about 1 hour.

Makes 8–12 servings.

Lobster Bisque

Treat yourself to this ultra-rich, decadent soup. To make a meal out of this, buy some lobster and cook it. Use the shells for the soup and put the meat on top of the soup. You can use shrimp shells instead of lobster shells, if you want, but the flavor is completely different.

3/4 cup vegetable or olive oil, divided
1 carrot, peeled and rough-chopped
5 stalks celery, rough-chopped
1 large yellow onion, rough-chopped
1 bulb raw garlic, skins removed
5 pounds of lobster shells (or shells from shrimp or crawfish)
1 tablespoon dried thyme
1 tablespoon dried basil
1 tablespoon dried oregano
1 tablespoon dried tarragon
1 teaspoon salt
1 tablespoon honey
1 can (16 ounces) diced or puréed tomatoes
1 1/2 gallons water
3 tablespoons soup base (vegetable or chicken)
1/2 pound (2 sticks) butter
2 cups flour
2 cups heavy cream
Cooked lobster meat (optional)

Preheat oven to 350 degrees. Combine 1/2 cup of oil with the carrots, celery, onion, garlic, and lobster shells in a large roasting pan. Toss to coat mixture completely with oil. Roast the vegetable-shell mixture in the oven until shells are bright red and the vegetables are beginning to brown, about 30 minutes.

Combine thyme, basil, oregano, tarragon, salt, and honey in a small mixing bowl.

Heat the remaining 1/4 cup oil in a 2- to 3-gallon stockpot over medium-high flame. Add the vegetable-shell mixture and sauté for 2 minutes, stirring frequently. Add the spice-honey mixture and sauté for 5 minutes more.

Add tomatoes, water, and soup base to the stockpot mixture. Simmer until you have reduced the amount of liquid by one-third. DO NOT BOIL IT, because you won't develop any flavor that way.

Allow the soup to cool a bit. Pick out as many lobster shells as you can, using a pair of tongs. Leave all of the vegetables in the soup. Using a hand-held blender, purée the soup in the stockpot (or purée it in batches in a food processor). Strain the soup through a fine-mesh sieve to get rid of any leftover shells. Use the back of a wooden spoon to push all of the liquid through. Return sieved mixture to the stockpot.

Make a roux: Melt butter in a medium saucepan. Stir in the flour. Cook over low heat, stirring often, until the flour begins to take on a light, nutty aroma, about 15 minutes.

Add the heavy cream to the mixture in the stockpot and bring it back to a simmer. Add the roux to thicken the soup, a little at a time. The key here is to stir and blend the soup while adding the roux and bringing the soup back up to a simmer. This causes the roux to thicken to its maximum. Add until the consistency is as you like it.

Garnish each serving with lobster meat, if desired.

Makes 10 or more servings.

3 Easy Rules

I've been cooking a long time. It is the only thing that has ever seemed right for me. I've learned many valuable lessons while standing next to a stove. Here are three.

1. **Start** with **good quality** ingredients.

2. Go for **simple**, straightforward **flavor**. It doesn't make sense to add so many seasonings that you can't tell **what's what**.

3. Use **simple cooking** techniques.

Mushroom Barley Soup

1/4 pound (1 stick) butter
1 carrot, peeled and diced
5 stalks celery, diced
1 large yellow onion, diced
1 tablespoon minced fresh garlic
2 pounds button, crimini, or portobello mushrooms, chopped
1 teaspoon dried basil
1 teaspoon dried oregano
1 teaspoon dried rosemary
2 teaspoons dried thyme
1 tablespoon soup base (vegetable or chicken)
1/4 cup flour
1 can (16 ounces) chopped tomatoes
1 1/2 cups pearl barley
1 gallon water
1 tablespoon salt
1 teaspoon black pepper

Heat the butter in a 2- to 3-gallon stockpot over medium heat. Add the carrots and sauté them until they start to soften, about 5 minutes. Add the celery and cook until softened, 3 more minutes. Add the onion and garlic to the stockpot and sauté until the onion is translucent.

Add the mushrooms, spices, and soup base to the stockpot. Sauté the mixture until the mushrooms begin to release their liquid. This is the major flavoring for the soup.

Add the flour to the stockpot. Stir to combine and cook for 5 minutes. Add tomatoes, barley, water, salt, and pepper to the stockpot. Simmer until the barley is tender, 40–50 minutes.

Makes 8–12 servings.

Tomato Basil Soup

1/3 cup vegetable or olive oil
3 stalks celery, chopped small
1/2 large yellow onion, chopped small
2 tablespoons minced fresh garlic
2 tablespoons light brown sugar
1 tablespoon dried thyme
1 tablespoon dried oregano
2 tablespoons dried basil
1 tablespoon soup base (vegetable or chicken)
2 cans (each 16 ounces) puréed tomatoes
1 quart water
2 cups heavy cream
Salt and pepper
Crusty French bread

Heat vegetable or olive oil in a 2–3 gallon stockpot over medium heat. Add celery, onion, and garlic and sauté, stirring occasionally, until onion is caramelized (lightly browned).

Add brown sugar, thyme, oregano, basil, and soup base to the stockpot and sauté 5 more minutes.

Add the tomatoes, water and cream to the mixture. Simmer for approximately 1 hour, stirring occasionally. Remove from heat and let cool to lukewarm.

Purée the soup mixture until smooth with a hand blender in the stockpot (or in batches in a food processor). Reheat. Season with salt and pepper to taste. Serve warm with crusty French bread.

Makes 6–8 servings.

Tomato Chicken Tarragon Soup

This soup is our most popular and most requested soup. I make it at least twice a week in ten-gallon batches.

1/3 cup vegetable or olive oil
2 large carrots, peeled and diced small
5 stalks celery, diced small
1 large yellow onion, diced small
2 tablespoons minced fresh garlic
2 tablespoons dried thyme
1 tablespoon dried oregano
1 tablespoon dried basil
2 tablespoons dried tarragon
2 tablespoons soup base (vegetable or chicken)
2 tablespoons light brown sugar
1 pound (about 2 cups) cooked, chopped chicken
4 cans (each 16 ounces) puréed tomatoes
2 quarts water
1 quart heavy cream
1 tablespoon salt
1 teaspoon black pepper
Freshly grated Parmesan
Homemade croutons

Heat the vegetable or olive oil in a 2–3 gallon stockpot over medium heat. Add the carrots and sauté them, stirring occasionally, for about 5 minutes. When they begin to soften, add the celery and sauté until tender; about 3 more minutes. Add the onion and garlic. Sauté until the onion is translucent.

Add thyme, oregano, basil, tarragon, soup base, brown sugar, and chicken. Cook for 5 minutes.

Add the tomatoes, water, heavy cream, salt, and pepper; simmer for approximately 30 minutes.

Serve with freshly grated Parmesan cheese and homemade croutons.

Makes 16 servings—and you will want even more!

Carrot Ginger Soup

1/3 cup vegetable or olive oil
2 1/2 pounds carrots, chopped
2 1/2 stalks celery, chopped
1/2 large yellow onion, chopped
1 tablespoon minced fresh garlic
1 tablespoon dried thyme
2 teaspoons dried oregano
2 tablespoons soup base (vegetable or chicken)
1 tablespoon dried ginger
2 teaspoons Chinese Five-Spice Blend (page 55)
1 tablespoon honey
2 quarts water
1/2 cup heavy cream
Salt and pepper to taste

Heat vegetable or olive oil in a 2- or 3-gallon stockpot. Add carrots, celery, and onion and sauté until vegetables are tender, stirring occasionally, about 10 minutes.

Add garlic, thyme, oregano, soup base, ginger, Chinese five-spice, and honey. Sauté for about 5 minutes.

Add water and cream to the mixture. Simmer, stirring occasionally, for about 30 minutes.

Remove soup from heat and let cool.

Using a food processor or hand blender in the stockpot, purée the soup until completely smooth. Reheat to serve.

Makes about 2 1/2 quarts, about 8 servings.

Carrot Ginger Soup *garnished with* Roasted Poblano Purée *(page 42) and fried carrot chip*

SALADS
& Dressings

Grilled Ratatouille Salad

Ratatouille is a vegetable stew, but it also makes a great spring or summer salad. This salad doesn't have a dressing. I let the flavors of the vegetables tossed with olive oil and vinegar do the work.

1 eggplant, cut into large matchsticks
2 zucchini, cut into large matchsticks
2 yellow squash, cut into large matchsticks
2 medium red onions, cut into 6 wedges each
1/4 cup extra-virgin olive oil, divided
Salt and pepper
2 cloves roasted garlic*
2 tablespoons balsamic vinegar
1/2 pound mixed greens, or 1 large head chopped lettuce
1/4 cup finely chopped basil
1 teaspoon crushed red pepper flakes
3 roasted red peppers, skins removed and flesh chopped (page 42)
5 tomatoes, sliced

Fire up the grill.

Toss the eggplant, zucchini, yellow squash, and onions with a little bit of the olive oil in a mixing bowl. Season them with salt and pepper. Grill them until they are softened. Cool in the refrigerator.

In another bowl, add the remaining olive oil, roasted garlic, and balsamic vinegar; mash this all into a paste. Add the lettuce, basil, and red pepper flakes. Toss to combine, then add the roasted red peppers, grilled eggplant, zucchini, yellow squash, and onion.

To serve, place the vegetables and greens in the middle of a plate. Arrange tomato slices around the rim.

Makes 4 dinner-sized salads.

*To roast garlic, wrap unpeeled cloves of garlic in aluminum foil. Bake at 350 degrees for 1 hour. Squeeze the softened flesh from the peels. Then you can measure out what you need.

Tortilla Salad

This comes as a side dish with all of our enchiladas. We also add it to salads and as a side to grilled fish or chicken.

Tip: A really helpful tool for this recipe is a mandolin. If you cut a lot of really thin slices, spend the money and buy a good one. Like a good knife, it will last forever.

1 bag of tortilla chips (your favorite kind), broken up a bit
1 jicama, julienned as thinly as possible
1 medium red pepper, cut into thin strips
1 poblano pepper, cut into thin strips
1 medium red onion, sliced as thinly as possible
Chopped fresh cilantro
Sliced green onions
Chipotle vinaigrette

Chipotle Vinaigrette

I love this dressing. I use it for salads, sandwiches, and sauces on all sorts of preparations. It's sweet, smoky, and a little spicy. What more could you ask for? This dressing is a classic example of an emulsified dressing—that means spices and flavors are dispersed and suspended in oil. Take care to keep it cool, as heat will cause the ingredients to separate.

1 tablespoon canned puréed chipotle
    in adobo sauce
2 tablespoons honey
1 teaspoon Dijon mustard
1 cup vegetable oil

Combine chipotle, honey, and mustard in a processor or blender and purée the mixture. Slowly pour the oil into the food processor while it is running.

Makes 1 cup.

Toss the ingredients in a big bowl. Wait until the last minute to toss this, or it will get soggy.

Makes 8–12 servings, unless it's for my friends Cory and Chris, then it makes 2.

Turkey Waldorf Salad

This is a great salad for a hot summer day. Try it on mixed greens or a croissant.

1/2 medium red onion, minced
1/2 bunch green onions, thinly sliced
1 stalk celery, minced
1/2 cup plain yogurt
1/2 cup sour cream
Zest and juice of 1/2 lemon*
1/2 pound fire-roasted grapes
1 cup candied walnuts
1/2 pound diced cooked turkey
Salt and pepper to taste

Combine all ingredients and mix well.

Makes enough for 4–6 sandwiches or salads.

*To zest, grate the yellow peel of the lemon with a fine grater. Don't grate the white pith; it's bitter.

Fire-Roasted Grapes

Fire-roasting grapes intensifies their natural sweetness.

Put the grapes, still in the bunch and on the stems, on the grill or over the flame on a gas stove. Turn them with tongs and grill them until the skins are charred. You can also use a torch.

That's it.

Candied Walnuts

1 cup walnuts
1/4 cup honey
1 teaspoon salt

Toast the nuts in a dry saucepan and when good and toasted—about 5 minutes—pour them into a bowl with honey and sprinkle with salt. Spread them out on cookie sheet to cool.

Makes 1 cup.

Tomato Cucumber Salad

This is a great side dish for grilled shrimp or scallops. It's quick and easy and it won't heat your kitchen up during the summer.

2/3 cup extra-virgin olive oil
1/4 cup rice wine vinegar
1 pinch of salt
1 pinch of pepper
1 teaspoon honey
2 beefsteak tomatoes, sliced as thin as possible. (Did you buy a mandolin yet?)
1 cucumber, sliced as thin as you can

Whisk the oil, vinegar, salt, pepper, and honey in a large bowl. Add the tomatoes and cucumbers. Cover and let this sit in the refrigerator for about an hour before serving.

Makes 2–4 servings.

Chicken Apple Walnut Salad

You can use the leftovers from the Herb Roasted Chicken recipe (page 100) in this salad. Top a plate of mixed greens with it, or slather it on multi-grain or wheat bread for a yummy sandwich.

Meat from one 2–3 pound roasted chicken, but no skin
1 celery rib, minced
1/2 medium red onion, minced
1 teaspoon fresh garlic, minced
1/2 cup Gorgonzola cheese (blue cheese will work)
1/2 cup toasted walnuts
1 apple, with skin, diced
6 basil leaves, chopped
2 cups mayonnaise
1/2 cup buttermilk
2 green onions, sliced
1/2 teaspoon salt
1 pinch pepper

Put the chicken, celery, red onion, garlic, cheese, walnuts, apple, and basil in a medium-sized bowl. Toss to combine completely.

Combine the mayonnaise, buttermilk, green onions, salt, and pepper in a separate bowl. Fold the mayonnaise mixture into the chicken mixture. Refrigerate for at least one hour before serving.

Makes enough for 8–10 sandwiches or salads.

Asian Slaw

Man-oh-man do we go through a lot of this at Bluephies on sandwiches, salads, tacos, pastas, and side dishes. I am still trying to figure out how to make a dessert from this yummy slaw.

1 napa cabbage, thinly sliced
1 head bok choy, thinly sliced (all of it)
1 medium red onion, thinly sliced
1 carrot, cut into thin matchsticks
1 red pepper, thinly sliced
1/4 head purple cabbage, thinly sliced

Asian Dressing
2 tablespoons sesame oil
1 medium red onion, chopped
1 tablespoon minced fresh garlic
1 tablespoon minced fresh ginger
1 cup sherry wine
1/3 cup rice wine vinegar
1/3 cup white vinegar
1 cup hoisin sauce (Asian sweet-sour, slightly spicy sauce)
2 cups vegetable oil
1/2 cup Mae Ploy (Thai sweet chile sauce)

Use a mandolin to cut the vegetables, or do it by hand with a sharp knife. A food processor will turn the vegetables into mush. After preparing all vegetables, place them all together in a large mixing bowl and toss.

To make the dressing: Heat the sesame oil in a medium-sized saucepan. Add the onion, garlic, and ginger and sauté, stirring occasionally, until the onion starts to caramelize. Add the sherry, rice wine vinegar, and white vinegar. Bring to a strong simmer and cook until the liquid is reduced by half. This will concentrate the flavors.

Remove the saucepan from heat and let it cool until you can put a finger in without burning it. (Try to use someone else's finger.) Add the onion mixture to a food processor. Add the hoisin sauce and turn the processor on to purée. Slowly drizzle the vegetable oil into the processor to emulsify the dressing.

For each serving, combine 2–3 cups of the prepared Asian greens with 1/4 cup of Asian Dressing. Add 2 tablespoons Mae Ploy. Toss the ingredients and coat thoroughly. It's that easy.

Serve as a side in place of a vegetable on your plate. It's also great in stir-fries, egg rolls, and spring rolls.

Makes 8 or more servings, but it can vary depending on the size of the cabbage and bok choy.

Rice Tabouli Salad

You can use different grains and come up with similar results. Bulgur is the most commonly used grain for tabouli.

2 cups uncooked white rice
1 cucumber, seeded and diced
2 tomatoes, diced
1 medium red onion, diced
1 tablespoon minced fresh garlic
3 tablespoons chopped basil
1 tablespoon salt
1 teaspoon black pepper
1/4 cup lemon juice
1/2 cup extra-virgin olive oil

Cook the rice according to the instructions on the package, and then cool it in the fridge or under cold running water. (If you do the latter, drain it well after rinsing.)

Mix the cucumbers, tomatoes, onion, garlic, basil, salt, pepper, lemon juice, and olive oil in a large bowl. Add the chilled rice and toss to combine thoroughly.

Makes 4–6 large servings.

Avocado Ranch Dressing

1 teaspoon minced fresh garlic
1/2 teaspoon salt
1 cup mayonnaise
1/4 cup buttermilk
3 tablespoons chopped flat-leaf parsley
4 chives, snipped
1 green onion, finely diced
1 teaspoon white vinegar
1 pinch black pepper
2 avocados, diced or puréed
1/2 medium sweet red pepper, diced

Combine all ingredients in a medium-sized bowl. Stir to combine evenly.

Refrigerated, it will keep for a week.

Makes just under 2 cups.

Lemon Vinaigrette

1/4 cup rice wine vinegar
Zest and juice of 2 lemons*
1 teaspoon dried basil
1 teaspoon dried thyme
1 teaspoon dried oregano
1 teaspoon salt
1/4 cup honey
1/2 cup olive oil
1/2 cup vegetable oil

Use a food processor, hand-held blender or—if you are really ambitious—a whisk.

Combine the vinegar, juice of the lemons, herbs, salt, and honey; process until well-blended. Continue to process as you slowly pour in the oils. (You can mix the oils ahead of time or add them separately.) When mixture has thickened, stir in the lemon zest.

Makes about 1 3/4 cups.

*To zest, grate the yellow peel of the lemon with a fine grater. Don't grate the white pith; it's bitter.

Chunky Gorgonzola Dressing

I like to substitute Gorgonzola for blue cheese. It's more expensive but I like the intense flavor.

1 cup sour cream
1 cup mayonnaise
1 cup buttermilk
1 1/2 teaspoons pepper
1/2 teaspoon salt
1/2 teaspoon minced fresh garlic
1/4 cup minced fresh chives
1 cup Gorgonzola cheese

Add all the ingredients, except the cheese and chives, to a medium-sized bowl. Stir to combine or use a food processor. Then mix in the cheese and chives and let sit for at least an hour before serving so the flavors blend. Keep refrigerated.

Makes a tad over 4 cups.

Rice Wine Vinaigrette

This vinaigrette makes a great sauce for flaky white fish, in addition to dressing your favorite salad.

2 teaspoons fresh ginger root, minced
1 small shallot, minced
1 teaspoon minced fresh garlic
1/2 cup rice wine vinegar
1 teaspoon salt
1 cup vegetable oil

Combine ginger, shallot, garlic, vinegar, and salt in a stainless steel mixing bowl. Slowly drizzle the oil into the bowl while whisking the vinegar mixture.

For a kick, add 1 tablespoon minced fresh cilantro, or add 1 teaspoon crushed red pepper flakes.

Makes about 1 1/2 cups.

Sun-Dried Tomato Basil Balsamic Vinaigrette

2 teaspoons minced sun-dried tomatoes
2 tablespoons chopped fresh basil
1 teaspoon minced fresh garlic
1/4 cup balsamic vinegar
1 teaspoon honey
1 cup extra-virgin olive oil

Combine tomatoes, basil, garlic, vinegar, and honey in a medium bowl. Whisk until completely blended. Slowly drizzle in the olive oil while whisking to blend the ingredients.

Note: this dressing has a tendency to separate when sitting, so stir it before you use it. You can also add all the ingredients to a sealed jar and shake it until all ingredients are blended.

Makes about 1 1/4 cups.

Tortilla Salad with Chipotle Vinaigrette *(page 16) over* Black Bean Corn Relish *(page 74)*

Sesame Soy Dressing

1 green onion, chopped
1/2 teaspoon minced fresh garlic
1 teaspoon minced fresh cilantro
1 tablespoon tahini
1 tablespoon soy sauce
3 tablespoons Mae Ploy (Thai sweet chile sauce)
1 teaspoon sugar
1/2 cup sesame oil
1/2 cup vegetable oil

Combine green onion, garlic, cilantro, tahini, soy sauce, Mae Ploy, sugar, and sesame oil in a mixing bowl. Whisk to combine. Slowly drizzle in the oil while whisking, until completely blended. You can also use a food processor to make a smooth dressing.

Makes about 1 1/2 cups.

MARINADES
& Sauces

Basil Pesto

There are some really good pre-made pestos out on the market today, but this is simple. Make it fresh—the flavor will be much better. You can use all basil if you want, but using some spinach will cut down the cost.

You will need your food processor for this recipe.

1 ounce fresh basil, no stems (1 cup, loosely packed)
1 ounce baby spinach, stems are okay (1 cup, loosely packed)
1 teaspoon minced fresh garlic
1/4 cup toasted pine nuts or walnuts*
1/4 cup grated Parmesan cheese
1/4 cup extra-virgin olive oil

Combine all the ingredients in a food processor, except the olive oil. When they are chopped and smooth, add the oil. Let it go until it becomes a paste.

That's it. I don't add any salt; the cheese will provide the saltiness. Pepper is not necessary either.

Makes enough for 3–4 servings of pasta.

*Toast the nuts at 350 degrees for about 5 minutes.

Lemon Pesto

This will use up all that basil you planted. Try it on grilled vegetables or pasta.

1 1/2 ounces fresh basil, no stems (1 1/2 cups, loosely packed)
1/4 cup toasted walnuts or pine nuts*
1/4 cup grated Parmesan cheese
1/2 teaspoon minced fresh garlic
1/4 cup extra-virgin olive oil
1 lemon, zested**
Juice from 1/2 a lemon (use the zested one)

Chop all the ingredients in a food processor. Add the oil. Add the lemon zest and juice; blend to combine.

Makes enough for 3 pasta servings.

*Toast nuts at 350 degrees for about 5 minutes.

**To zest, grate the yellow peel with a fine greater and set aside. Don't grate the white pith; it's bitter.

Sun-Dried Tomato Pesto

1 1/2 ounces fresh basil, no stems (1 1/2 cups, loosely packed)
1/4 cup toasted walnuts or pine nuts
1/4 cup grated Parmesan cheese
1/2 teaspoon minced fresh garlic
1/4 cup sun-dried tomatoes (if you can ONLY find oil-packed tomatoes,
*   cut the olive oil in half)*
3/4 cup extra virgin-olive oil

Chop all of the ingredients except the olive oil in a food processor. When all the ingredients are chopped, add the oil and blend to combine.

Makes enough for 3 servings of pasta.

*Toast nuts in oven at 350 degrees for about 5 minutes.

Roasted Red Pepper Pesto

1 1/2 ounces fresh basil, no stems (1 1/2 cups, loosely packed)
1/4 cup toasted walnuts or pine nuts*
1/4 cup grated Parmesan cheese
1/2 teaspoon minced fresh garlic
1/4 cup extra-virgin olive oil
Zest and juice of 1 lemon**
1 roasted red pepper, charred, skin and seeds removed (page 42)

Combine all the ingredients except the olive oil and lemon zest in a food processor. When everything is chopped and blended, add the oil. Then add the lemon zest; blend to combine.

Makes enough for 3 servings of pasta.

*Toast the nuts at 350 degrees for about 5 minutes.

**To zest, grate the yellow peel of the lemon with a fine grater. Don't grate the white pith; it's bitter.

Pesto & Smoked Mozzarella Alfredo Sauce

Toss this sauce with grilled mushrooms, chicken, roasted red peppers, and noodles.

4 tablespoons butter
1/2 large yellow onion, diced
1 tablespoon roasted garlic*
1/4 cup flour
2 cups heavy cream
1 cup water
2 tablespoons lemon juice, freshly squeezed or bottled
2 teaspoons salt
1/2 teaspoon black pepper
1/4 cup Basil Pesto (page 29)
1 cup shredded smoked mozzarella

Melt the butter in a 2- to 3-gallon stockpot over medium heat. Add the onion and sauté until lightly browned and translucent.

Add the roasted garlic and cook for about 5 minutes. Reduce heat to low, add the flour to the sauté mixture, and cook for about 5 minutes more.

Add the heavy cream, water, lemon juice, salt, and pepper to the stockpot. Raise heat to medium and cook until the liquid is just about to simmer. Stir in the pesto and bring back to a simmer. Add the smoked mozzarella to the mixture and stir until melted. You can also purée until smooth with a hand blender.

Makes enough sauce for about 8 servings of pasta.

*To roast garlic, wrap unpeeled cloves of garlic in aluminum foil. Bake for 1 hour at 350 degrees. Squeeze the softened flesh from the peels. Then you can measure out what you need.

Ginger Soy Sauce

This light sauce works well with any mild-flavored seafood or chicken. It goes perfectly with a simple grilled chicken breast, catfish filet, or other light, white fish. At Bluephies, we use this sauce a lot for any dish we put on sticky rice and sesame-seared vegetables.

1/2 bunch minced fresh chives
1 tablespoon plus 1 teaspoon minced fresh ginger
1 tablespoon minced fresh garlic
1/4 cup soy sauce
1/8 cup brown sugar
1/8 cup rice wine vinegar
1/8 cup Key lime juice (sweetened lime juice or fresh-squeezed will work as well)
1 tablespoon water

Add all of the ingredients to a mixing bowl. Stir to combine.

Kept refrigerated, the sauce will last for a couple of days.

Makes enough sauce for 4 servings.

Ancho Ginger Rub

This rub will give chicken and pork a nice sweet smoky flavor. Try to rub it on the meat at least 4 hours before you cook it. Like a marinade, it will work best if you give it some time. Also, when you cook it, let the meat form a crust before you turn it over.

1/4 cup ground ancho chile
2 teaspoons ground ginger
2 teaspoons salt
1/2 teaspoon black pepper

Add the spices together in a bowl and whisk to combine evenly.

Makes enough to coat 2 pounds of meat.

Mushroom Pasta Sauce

4 tablespoons butter
1/2 large yellow onion, diced
2 teaspoons minced fresh garlic
1 pound mushrooms (button, crimini, and portobello) cut into large pieces
1/2 teaspoon dried basil
1/2 teaspoon dried oregano
1/2 teaspoon dried rosemary
1 teaspoon dried thyme
2 teaspoons soup base (vegetable or chicken)
1/8 cup flour
1 can (16 ounces) diced tomatoes, or 2 large tomatoes, peeled and chopped
2 cups water
1 cup heavy cream

Melt the butter in a large saucepan over medium heat. Add onion and garlic; sauté until translucent. Add the mushrooms and sauté until they begin to release their natural liquid. This is the major flavoring for the sauce.

Add the basil, oregano, rosemary, thyme, and soup base. Sauté for 5 minutes. Add the flour and stir to combine. Cook for 5 minutes more, stirring occasionally.

Add the tomatoes, water, and heavy cream; simmer until the sauce has thickened.

Makes enough for 8 servings of pasta.

Honey Wasabi Sauce

This is a great sauce for meaty fish. I like to prepare fish the same way I do steaks, like this: Season the fish with a liberal amount of oil, salt, and pepper and either grill or sear it to medium-rare. This gives the fish a good flavor and texture on the out-side but brings the inside to a warm temperature and keeps the flavor intact. The meat also stays tender.

Note: not all fish should be cooked to medium and medium-rare. Trout, white-fish, and similar fish should be cooked through.

4 tablespoons honey
2 tablespoon wasabi

Combine the two ingredients in a small bowl. Heat it in a microwave or on the stovetop. Stir to combine. Get the lumps out or you will get a nice little hot surprise.

You can make more and keep it refrigerated for a long time. The honey won't spoil.

Makes 2 servings.

Rum Coconut Glaze

This glaze adds a tropical kick to chicken or mahi mahi.

1 can (14 ounces) coconut milk
1 small cinnamon stick
1/3 cup soy sauce
1/2 cup dark rum
1 tablespoon peppercorns

Bring the rum to a simmer in a large saucepan. The alcohol will evaporate, which will make a smoother sauce. Add the remaining ingredients and simmer until the sauce reduces to a syrup consistency. Strain through a fine-mesh strainer.

Makes enough glaze for 6 servings.

Five-Spice Soy Marinade

This is my favorite marinade for chicken, pork, and beef. It's the ultimate combination of salty and sweet. What more can you ask for? Spend the money for a good quality soy sauce, you can really taste the difference. (Low-sodium doesn't taste as good.)

1/2 cup soy sauce
2 tablespoon honey
2 tablespoon Chinese Five-Spice Blend (page 55)
2 tablespoon Mae Ploy (Thai sweet chili sauce)

Combine all the ingredients in a bowl. Stir well.

Marinate meat in this sauce several hours, or overnight if you can, in the refrigerator. When you cook it, the sugars in the marinade caramelize and create a dramatic depth of flavor.

For a really good sauce, bring the marinade to a boil in a saucepan. Stir in a teaspoon of butter. A good ratio is one batch of sauce for every two people, or double it if you like sauce like I do.

Makes enough marinade for 2 whole chicken breasts, or 2 small steaks, or 2 pork chops.

Chile Ginger Apple Marinade
(for Pork & Chicken)

This makes meat moist and flavor penetrate. If you substitute water for the apple juice, it will work well on salmon.

1/4 cup brown sugar
1/4 cup white sugar
1/8 teaspoon salt
1 teaspoon dried ground ginger
2 teaspoons ground ancho chile
2 cups apple juice

Combine all the ingredients in a large pan. Warm the mixture until the sugar dissolves. Let the liquid cool before you add the meat.

Marinate pork or chicken at least 4 hours in fridge; overnight would be better. If you're making salmon, don't marinate it for more than 2 hours.

Makes enough marinade for about 2 pounds of meat.

Caramelized Tomatillo Sauce

We serve this sauce with really hearty grilled fish, like tilapia or amberjack. It works great with soft-shell crabs too. This sauce is naturally sweet and it has a kick.

1 tablespoon vegetable oil
10 tomatillos, husks removed
1 large yellow onion, chopped
2 poblano peppers, chopped
1/4 jalapeño pepper, seeds removed

You can soak the tomatillos in warm water to help remove the husks.

Heat the oil on low-medium heat in a large saucepan. Add all the vegetables to the pan. Stir occasionally, but allow the vegetables to caramelize. After a while, the sugars in the vegetables start to come out and that's the flavor you're looking for. Be patient. Do not turn the heat up to quicken this process. You'll burn the vegetables.

When the vegetables are finished cooking, in about 20–25 minutes, purée the batch with a hand-held blender. Strain the purée through a fine-mesh strainer. Push it through with the back of a ladle. If you take out the seeds, it makes a nicer presentation.

Makes about 1 cup, depending on size of peppers and tomatillos.

Coconut-Chile Sauce

Charlie Lawson, a long-time cook at Bluephies, loves this stuff. We use it on many specials including chicken, calamari, and catfish dishes.

1 can (15 ounces) coconut milk
1 cup Mae Ploy (Thai sweet chili sauce)

Combine the two ingredients in a small saucepan. Simmer on medium heat until reduced by 1/3.

Makes 4 servings.

Diablo Verde Salsa

This spicy little green devil comes from one of my prep cooks. It's really simple but man is it hot! The first time he made it for me I tried a big spoonful of it and started running for a big glass of water! I eat it cold on chips, quesadillas, or grilled vegetables.

This is the tamed-down version.

1 quart water
1/2 cup vegetable oil
4 tablespoons salt
1 1/2 pounds tomatillos, husks removed
5 jalapeños
6 whole cloves garlic
1 bunch cilantro

Add the water, oil, salt, tomatillos, jalapeños, and garlic to a large saucepan. Boil for about 20 minutes. Add the cilantro and let it cool. Purée smooth with a hand blender or a food processor. Push the purée through a fine mesh strainer to strain out all of the jalapeños and tomatillos seeds.

Makes 4 cups.

Pineapple & Pickled Ginger Salsa

I especially like this with grilled meat. It's a fruit salsa that will compliment any spicy chicken, fish, pork, or turkey.

1 pineapple, peeled and sliced
1/4 cup sugar
1/2 cup rice wine vinegar
1 poblano pepper, diced
1 medium red pepper, diced
1 medium red onion, minced
1 green onion, thinly sliced
1 jalapeño, seeds removed and minced
1 tablespoon chopped pickled ginger
1 tablespoon chopped fresh cilantro

Grill half the pineapple, then cube it. While the pineapple is grilling, boil the sugar and vinegar together and reduce it by half. Cube the pineapple half you didn't grill.

Add the chopped vegetables, all the pineapple, ginger, and cilantro to the vinegar-sugar mixture and stir to combine. Let it cool.

Makes 4–6 servings.

Roasted Poblano Purée

We use this purée as a sauce on enchiladas. It adds flavor and it makes a really cool plate presentation. The color is vibrant and you can use the purée in squeeze bottles to make designs on the plate. The heat of peppers varies, so the heat level of this dish will depend on the peppers you use.

4 poblano peppers
1 tablespoon vegetable oil
1 teaspoon honey
1/8 cup water
Salt to taste

Roasting peppers: There are a few ways to roast peppers. This method will work no matter the color or size. Coat the peppers with vegetable oil. Place the peppers right on a hot grill or the flame on your stove. Use tongs to rotate them. Cook the peppers this way until they are black and blistered all over. You can also roast them in a hot oven.

Put the blackened peppers in a covered container. They will steam a little and the skin will loosen in about 20 minutes. Peel the skin away and remove the seeds. Rinse under water and that's it.

To make the purée, combine peppers, honey, water, and salt in a food processor; blend until smooth.

Makes about 2 cups.

Spinach Fontinella Cream Sauce

This is a tasty sauce for pasta or rice.

4 tablespoons butter
1/2 large yellow onion, diced
2 teaspoons minced fresh garlic
1/2 teaspoon dried thyme
1/2 teaspoon dried oregano
1/2 teaspoon dried basil
2 teaspoons lemon juice (freshly squeezed or bottled)
1 tablespoon mustard (Dijon or coarse-grain)
1 tablespoon soup base (vegetable or chicken)
2 teaspoons salt
1/2 teaspoon black pepper
1/4 cup flour
2 cups water
2 cups heavy cream
1 pound spinach
1/2 cup shredded Fontinella cheese

Melt butter in a large saucepan over medium heat. Add the onion and sauté until fragrant and translucent.

Add the garlic, thyme, oregano, and basil; sauté for 3 minutes. Add lemon juice, mustard, and soup base. Sauté until all ingredients are warm and well blended.

Add salt, pepper, and flour; stir to combine. Cook over medium-low heat for about 5 minutes, stirring regularly.

Add the water, cream, and spinach. Heat until the sauce begins to simmer. Stir in the cheese just before serving.

Makes enough sauce for about 8 servings of pasta.

Charred Tomato Salsa

This is a great accent for spicy marinated chicken or fish. Or just serve it with chips. I leave the seeds of the jalapeño in this salsa to give it some heat.

6 beefsteak tomatoes
1 medium red onion, peeled and cut in half
2 jalapeños, tops removed
1 tablespoon minced fresh garlic
1 teaspoon salt
Pinch of black pepper
Juice of 1 lime
1 tablespoon chopped fresh cilantro

Char the tomatoes on a grill or gas stove. They will look burned, but that's okay. Do the same thing with the onion and the jalapeños. (See the instructions for roasting peppers in the Roasted Poblano Purée recipe, page 42.)

Once all of the vegetables are charred, let them cool. Put them in a food processor with the garlic, salt, pepper, lime juice, and cilantro. Purée until smooth.

Makes about 5 cups.

Pineapple White Chocolate Mole

This is a fun twist on a traditional mole sauce. I put about every ingredient I could think of in here. This goes great with any grilled, meaty fish like mahi mahi .

1 quart vegetable stock
1 pineapple, skinned, cored, and chopped
1/3 cup dry sherry
1 cinnamon stick
1/4 cup raisins
1/4 teaspoon cumin
1 tablespoon ground ancho or 3 whole ancho chiles
1 large yellow onion, chopped
3 cloves garlic
1 jalapeño, seeded and chopped
1/4 cup slivered or sliced almonds
2 tablespoons tahini
1 cup tortilla chips
1 pinch of cloves
1 pinch of allspice
2 ounces white chocolate
1 tablespoon vegetable oil

Put the vegetable stock, pineapple, sherry, cinnamon stick, raisins, cumin, and ground (or whole) anchos in a big stockpot. Bring to a boil; let it boil for about 10 minutes.

Add the onion, garlic, jalapeño, almonds, tahini, and tortillas. Simmer until the sauce becomes the consistency of gravy. Purée this mixture with a hand-held blender. Add the cloves, allspice, and white chocolate.

Heat the mixture just enough to melt the chocolate, then strain through a fine-mesh strainer. You will have to push it through with the back of a wood spoon or ladle.

Now, here comes the tricky part—REFRY IT: Heat the vegetable oil in a large shallow sauté pan until it is very hot. Once the pan is super hot, pour in the sauce. WATCH OUT—it will splash and splatter. This step is important to finish the sauce and develop flavor.

Makes enough for about 8 servings.

Appetizers

& SIDE
DISHES

Baba Ganoush

This is a great spread for pita or crostini or as part of a salad sampler. I like the grilled flavor of this dish.

1 eggplant
2 tablespoons tahini
Zest and juice of 1/2 lemon, divided*
1 clove roasted garlic**
1 1/2 tablespoons extra-virgin olive oil
1 tablespoon sesame seeds

Peel the eggplant and slice it, then grill until soft. Set it aside until it's cool enough to handle. (If grilling is not an option, you can roast it in the oven.)

Place the eggplant in a food processor with tahini, lemon zest, garlic, half the lemon juice, and purée. Slowly pour in the olive oil with the machine still running.

Toast the sesame seeds over medium heat in a dry sauté pan until they turn a light gold color.

Pour the eggplant mixture out of the food processor and into a bowl. Stir in the toasted sesame seeds.

Makes about 2 cups.

*To zest, grate the yellow peel with a fine greater and set aside. Don't grate the white pith, it's bitter.

**To roast garlic, wrap unpeeled cloves of garlic in aluminum foil. Bake for 1 hour at 350 degrees. Squeeze the softened flesh from the peels. Then you can measure out what you need.

Baked Beans

I enjoy simple foods the most. I could eat baked beans every meal. They taste great the day they are made, and are even better the next day!

1 pound bacon, chopped
1 large yellow onion, chopped
2 tablespoons fresh garlic, minced
1/4 cup tomato paste
2 chipotle peppers in adobo, puréed (available in Mexican food aisle)
1/2 cup light brown sugar
1/4 cup molasses
1/4 cup yellow mustard
5 cups stock (vegetable, beef, or chicken)
1 pound dried white beans
1 tablespoon salt
1 teaspoon black pepper
1/2 teaspoon ground ancho chiles

Soak the beans overnight in just enough water to cover.

Preheat oven to 300 degrees.

Sauté the bacon in a large ovenproof thick bottom pot, until all the fat cooks out of the bacon and the meat is crisp. Add the onion and garlic; cook until translucent. Add the tomato paste.

Add the chipotle peppers, brown sugar, molasses and mustard. Cook for about 3 minutes. Add the stock.

Drain the soaked beans and add to the stockpot. Then add the salt, pepper, and ancho chiles. Stir to combine. Cover the pot and place in the oven. Cook for about 4 hours.

Makes 8 servings.

Caponata

This is an old-school dish made from eggplant, tomatoes, and olives. It is a great topping for pizza or crostini or as a garnish for lamb. We use kalamata olives in this recipe; other black olives will work, but you may have to adjust the saltiness, since kalamata olives have the perfect amount of salt for this dish.

1/4 cup olive oil
1 large yellow onion, diced
1 eggplant unpeeled, cubed
1 tablespoon minced fresh garlic
1 teaspoon dried thyme
1/4 teaspoon dried oregano
1/4 teaspoon dried basil
1/2 cup white wine
4 beefsteak tomatoes,
    cored and chopped
1 teaspoon capers
10 kalamata olives,
    pitted and chopped

Heat the olive oil in a large saucepan over medium heat. Add onion and sauté until translucent. That will take about 5 minutes. Add the eggplant and cook for another 5 minutes. Add the garlic, thyme, oregano, and basil. Cook until fragrant.

Add wine to deglaze the pan (scrape bits from bottom and sides of pan, and stir to make a sauce.) Then add the tomatoes, capers, and olives. Reduce the heat to low. Simmer until the tomatoes break apart and the mixture cooks down and becomes somewhat thick.

Makes about 1 quart.

Creamed Corn

You can't resist buying a dozen ears of corn when they're on sale, can you? Then you have to figure out how to use the leftovers. Here is a great solution. I like to make this on the grill.

6–8 ears of corn, husks removed (about 2 pounds of kernels)
3 tablespoons butter
1 teaspoon minced fresh garlic
1 shallot, minced (or use 1 really small minced onion)
1 tablespoon salt
1 teaspoon pepper
1/4 cup flour
1 1/4 cups heavy cream
1 pinch nutmeg
1/4 cup shredded Swiss cheese
1/4 cup grated Parmesan cheese

Fire up the grill and roast the ears of corn. It's okay if some of the corn gets kind of dark-colored. Just keep turning them so they don't burn.

Melt the butter in a cast iron pan. Add the garlic and shallots to the pan. Cook until the shallots are translucent. Add the salt and pepper. Add the flour. This makes a roux, which will thicken the corn mixture. Stir the mixture so the flour doesn't burn. Cook it for about 7 minutes.

Add the cream to the pan and whisk to incorporate. Make sure you get rid of all the lumps. Put in the pinch of nutmeg. Bring to a boil, then back the heat down to a simmer.

Cut the corn off the cob and place in a bowl. Stir half the cheese into the hot cream mixture and whisk until the cheese is melted. Add the corn and stir to combine. Top the corn with the rest of the cheese. Place pan on the grill and let the heat melt the cheese.

Makes 6–8 servings.

Chile-Infused Sweet Potatoes

These guys have become a staple in the restaurant.

4 average-sized sweet potatoes (unpeeled), washed and roasted
*   until soft*
1/2 teaspoon dried ginger
2 tablespoons Mae Ploy (Thai sweet chili sauce)
1/2 teaspoon black pepper
2 teaspoons salt

Blend all ingredients in an upright mixer on low until the potatoes are smashed. Or do it the old fashioned way—with a potato masher. Mmmmmm, good!

Makes 6 servings.

How to Roast Sweet Potatoes

Wash the sweet potatoes and put them in a 9 x 13-inch pan. Bake them uncovered in a 350-degree oven until they are soft. Big ones take longer than little ones, so choose the same sized potatoes if possible. Start checking them in about an hour.

When they're done they should be soft to the touch or, if you don't want to burn your fingers, you should be able to pierce them easily with a fork.

Crispy Fried Spinach

People should fry more food. It tastes so good. We use this as a garnish on some of our dishes, as well as just a side vegetable.

A little word of caution: there is a lot of water in spinach. And water in hot oil causes splashes. As long as you don't load up your fryer all at once, you will be fine.

I like to toss some spinach in the fryer when a new cook isn't paying attention then watch him react. The pops sound like firecrackers. That's my little job initiation.

1 handful of baby spinach (the big stuff won't work)
1/2 gallon vegetable oil
Salt

Heat the oil in a heavy-bottomed stockpot until the oil reaches 375 degrees. Use your trusty candy thermometer to get the right temperature.

Once at temperature, add the spinach to the oil and stand back. Let it pop away. Fry the spinach until it starts to float (about 2 minutes). When nearly done, gently move the spinach around with some metal tongs to make sure the oil is getting to all of the spinach.

Remove the spinach from the oil with a slotted spoon, drain on paper towels, and season with salt to taste.

Eggplant Caviar

This is a really simple dip that's great on baguettes. It's also a glimpse into how we cook at Bluephies. We don't always follow exact recipes. That's when cooking becomes a challenge. Try it; trust what you like and run with it.

1 eggplant, peeled and cubed
1/4 cup olive oil plus a little extra
Salt and pepper to taste
2 tablespoons water
1 shallot, finely minced or 1/2 small red onion, finely minced
1 clove roasted garlic*
Splash of balsamic vinegar

Preheat oven to 350 degrees.

Toss the eggplant with 1/4 cup of olive oil. Sprinkle with salt and pepper. Add a few splashes of water to the bowl and toss again. Spread the eggplant on a baking sheet and bake until the eggplant is soft, about 30 minutes.

Remove the eggplant from the oven and put it in a bowl. Add the minced shallot and garlic. Use the back of a fork to mash the eggplant, shallot, and garlic to a lumpy consistency. Add a splash of balsamic vinegar and the remaining olive oil. Stir the mixture, taste it, and add more oil, vinegar, salt, and pepper to taste.

Makes enough caviar for one baguette.

*To roast garlic, wrap unpeeled cloves of garlic in aluminum foil. Bake for 1 hour at 350 degrees. Squeeze the softened flesh from the peels. Then you can measure out what you need.

Spinach Au Gratin

16 ounces frozen spinach, thawed
1 1/2 cups shredded Cheddar cheese
3/4 cup red wine vinegar
1 cup heavy cream
1 cup panko bread crumbs (Japanese bread crumbs)
1 teaspoon salt
1 teaspoon black pepper

Preheat oven to 350 degrees.

Mix all ingredients together in a large bowl. Spray an oven proof-baking dish with non-stick spray and place gratin mix in the baking dish. Cover and bake for 15 minutes. Put the gratin in a cookie mold and press to shape.

Makes 4 servings.

Five-Spice Apples

This is a great side dish for pork, chicken, or fish and can be served warm or cold. It's kind of a dressed-up version of applesauce.

1 medium red onion, finely diced
1 teaspoon white sugar
1 teaspoon brown sugar
1 teaspoon Chinese Five-Spice Blend
1 cup apple juice
3 apples (unpeeled), cored and diced

Combine onion, both sugars, five-spice, and apple juice in a large saucepan. Bring to a boil and simmer for about 10 minutes. Add the diced apples and simmer until they are tender but retain their shape, 3–5 minutes.

Makes 4 servings.

Chinese Five-Spice Blend

I use Chinese Five-Spice Blend throughout this cookbook. A coffee bean grinder works perfectly for this but don't use your coffee grinder—buy another one—or your coffee will taste a little funny in the morning.

2 tablespoons whole black
*   peppercorns*
12 star anise
36 whole cloves
4 cinnamon sticks (about
*   2 tablespoons after ground)*
2 tablespoons fennel seed

Place all ingredients in the coffee grinder and grind to powder. You will have to do this in small batches. Store in an airtight container.

Yummy Polenta

I call this "hard polenta"—it starts out soft, then spreads and cooks down.
I serve it with braised dishes, like Lamb Shank Redemption (page 101) or Root Vegetable
Ragout (page 102). It takes a little prep time to get set up, but once that is done you can
bang this out at the last minute. It's one of those professional touches that will impress
your friends.

I love the flavor of either grilled or pan-fried polenta—crispy on the outside and
soft on the inside. It's yummy.

1 large yellow onion, finely diced
1 stalk celery, finely diced
3 tablespoons butter
1 tablespoon dried thyme
1 tablespoon dried oregano
1 teaspoon dried rosemary
6 cups vegetable stock*
1/2 cup shredded Parmesan cheese
3 cups medium cornmeal

Spray a 9 x 9-inch pan with non-stick spray. Place a piece of parchment paper
or plastic film on the bottom of the pan. Set aside.

Heat butter in a stockpot over medium flame. Add the onion and celery and
sauté until the onion becomes translucent. Add the spices and vegetable stock to the
mixture and bring to a boil. Once boiling, stir in the cheese and bring back to a boil. This
ensures the cheese is well incorporated into the dish.

Turn the heat to low and stir in the cornmeal slowly, a little at a time. If you add
the cornmeal too quickly, it will get lumpy. It's important to stir this dish continuously.
Cook on low heat until it's thick.

Pour the polenta out onto the lined pan. Spread it evenly. Put plastic over the
polenta to keep it from drying out. Place in the refrigerator to cool.

Once the polenta is cool and hard, use your favorite cookie cutter to cut out the
shapes you want. Grill or pan-fry the polenta.

Makes 6 servings plus some leftovers for other dishes.

Tip: You can save the scraps and make croutons for salads. It's easy—just cut the
scraps into a uniform size and toss with just enough oil to make the seasoning stick. You

can add 1/2 teaspoon each of thyme and oregano for an Italian flavor, or try 1/2 tea-spoon each of cumin and coriander for a Southwestern flair. Bake at 350 degrees until firm and crunchy on the outside, but a little soft on the inside.

Or you can grill the polenta scraps and then dry them in the oven. Use them for stuffing in place of bread. Here's how you do it: Fire up the ol' grill and toss the polenta in oil. Grill until you get good char marks. Put in the oven and dry on low heat—about 200 degrees. If it's not drying, grind it into smaller pieces and put it back in the oven until it's dry. You could make this stuffing for Thanksgiving dinner next year in place of bread stuffing.

*Note on vegetable stock: You can use a bouillon cube if you don't have stock. Use one cube and then replace the amount of stock with water. Or, if your stock is kind of bland, throw in a bouillon cube anyway to give it more flavor.

Olivada

Spread this on sourdough bread. It's also great on crostini with goat cheese.

2 cups pitted kalamata olives
1/4 cup extra-virgin olive oil
1 teaspoon fresh rosemary
1 teaspoon fresh thyme
1 teaspoon fresh oregano
1 teaspoon minced fresh garlic
1 teaspoon lemon juice
1/4 cup finely minced medium red onion
2 tablespoons capers

Purée the olives, oil, herbs, garlic, and lemon juice in a food processor. Transfer the mix to a large bowl. Stir in the onion and capers.

Makes about 2 cups.

Hummus

2 cups garbanzo beans, canned (drain and rinse) or cook your own
2 tablespoons olive oil
2 tablespoons lemon juice
2 tablespoons tahini
1 1/2 teaspoons salt
1 pinch black pepper
1/4 teaspoon ground cumin
1/2 teaspoon ground coriander
1 teaspoon minced fresh garlic
2 green onions, chopped
1 tablespoon minced fresh cilantro

Combine the beans, oil, lemon juice, tahini, salt, pepper, cumin, coriander, and garlic in a food processor. Purée until smooth. It will have a creamy texture and appearance. Remove the purée and place in a bowl. Stir in the cilantro and green onions.

Serve this on pita bread or crostini, or as part of a salad.

Makes about 2 cups.

Pickled Corn Relish

This is a tangy addition to Black Bean Soup (page 3), enchiladas, and quesadillas. Or, I just eat it by the spoonful.

The base flavor of this sauce is a traditional gastrique—that is, caramelized sugar deglazed with vinegar. I've simplified it for home cooks by just boiling it.

1 cup corn kernels, (frozen, canned or fresh)
1/2 poblano pepper, minced (green pepper will work as well)
1/2 medium red pepper, minced
1/4 medium red onion, minced
2 teaspoons minced fresh garlic
1 cup apple cider vinegar
1 cup sugar
1 green onion, minced
2 tablespoons minced fresh cilantro

Combine the corn, poblano pepper, red pepper, onion, garlic, vinegar, and sugar in a small saucepan; bring to a boil. Turn down the heat and simmer until the liquid has pretty much evaporated.

Stir in the green onion and cilantro. Turn off the heat and let the mixture cool before serving.

Makes about 1 cup, or enough garnishes for 6–8 enchiladas.

Pommes Frites

These are classic bistro French fries. They are so good that you won't want any ketchup.

Tip: If you want really thin fries, cut the potatoes into thin matchsticks for shoestring fries. These make a good garnish.

1/2 gallon vegetable oil
4 good-sized potatoes
2 tablespoons butter
1 tablespoon minced fresh garlic
Salt to taste
1 tablespoon chopped flat-leaf parsley
Coarse-cracked black pepper to taste

Heat the oil to 325 degrees in a heavy-bottomed saucepan. Use your candy thermometer to take the temperature.

While this is heating, cut your potatoes (skin on is okay) into strips about 1/2 inch square. Pat the potatoes dry with a paper towel to get rid of some of the excess moisture.

Heat the butter and garlic on low until the butter is melted and warm.

Fry the potatoes in the hot oil a few at a time, until they are soft and brown, about 3 minutes. Remove from heat with a slotted spoon and drain on paper towels. Season them with salt as soon as you put them on the paper towel. This helps to keep the salt on them.

After all of your potatoes are fried once, heat the oil up to 375 degrees. Add your potatoes back into the oil a few at a time and fry them for about 3 more minutes, until crispy. Transfer them to a bowl using a slotted spoon. Fry up the remaining potatoes.

At the last minute, add the parsley to the garlic butter mixture and then pour it over the potatoes. Grind some coarse-cracked black pepper over them and toss to mix.

You can save the oil and reuse it for about a week. Let it cool to room temperature in the pan. Pour it into an airtight jar. Seal it and put it in the refrigerator.

Makes 4 servings.

Scalloped Potatoes

Mom made these all the time, but it wasn't until I started cooking for a living that I made them myself. You can dress them up by using fancy potatoes like Yukon Golds or Kennebecs. Make a meal out of it by adding some vegetables or meat, or both. I like to make this as a base layer and put cooked shredded meat on top.

3 tablespoons butter
1/2 large yellow onion, minced or sliced as thin as possible
Salt and pepper to taste
3 tablespoons flour
1 cup heavy cream
3 large potatoes (skin on), sliced as thin as possible
1 cup shredded cheese (Swiss, mozzarella or Cheddar will work)

Preheat oven to 350 degrees.

Melt the butter in a medium saucepan. Add the onion and cook until tender. Season with salt and pepper. Add the flour and cook for another 5 minutes. Once the flour is incorporated, add the cream and whisk to completely get rid of the lumps. Bring this to a boil. Once boiling, remove from heat.

Spread a layer of the sauce on the bottom of a large baking dish. Arrange some of the potatoes in a thin layer in the pan. Sprinkle some cheese over the potatoes. Repeat with more layers of sauce, potatoes, and cheese, while alternating the direction of the potatoes with each layer. End with a cheese layer on top.

Cover with plastic wrap and then foil. Bake until the potatoes are fork tender, about 45 minutes.

Makes 4–6 servings.

Tomatillo Corn Relish

1 medium red onion
1 red pepper
15 tomatillos, husks removed
2/3 cup apple cider vinegar
1/3 cup sugar
1 cup corn kernels (frozen or canned)
1 teaspoon minced fresh garlic

Dice the red onion, red pepper, and 10 of the tomatillos to the size of the corn kernels. This makes a good presentation.

Place all cut vegetables in a small saucepan. Add the vinegar and sugar; boil until the liquid has almost evaporated.

Char the remaining tomatillos on your grill or stove top. Rotate them with tongs in the flame until completely charred; let cool. Chop the charred tomatillos and add to the saucepan. Add the corn and garlic. Cook for a few more minutes. Let cool and start eating. This is great on tacos, grilled fish or chicken.

Makes about 2 cups.

Tomato Olive Butter

We serve this butter with our sourdough bread. This butter has a rather addictive quality. It works best if you make this recipe in an upright mixer. The recipe makes a lot, but you can cut it in half.

1 pound unsalted butter, at room temperature
4 ounces cream cheese, at room temperature
1/4 teaspoon minced fresh garlic
1/8 teaspoon salt
1 teaspoon Cajun Spices
1 teaspoon dried parsley
4–5 halves of re-hydrated sun-dried tomatoes*
6–7 kalamata olives, pitted and chopped

Combine the butter and cream cheese in a mixing bowl and blend until smooth. Add the remaining ingredients all at once with the mixer still running. Mix until evenly distributed. If you don't have a mixer, mash with a fork until blended.

The butter is ready to eat, but keep the remaining butter refrigerated. Before serving, it's best to let the butter soften at room temperature. Don't put the compound butter in the microwave or on the stovetop to speed softening. The ingredients will separate.

Makes about 2 1/2 cups.

*To re-hydrate sun dried tomatoes, steep in hot water for 10–15 minutes.

Cajun Spices

1/4 cup kosher salt
1/3 cup cayenne pepper
1/4 cup paprika
1/4 cup granulated garlic
   or garlic powder
1/4 cup ground black pepper
1 tablespoon granulated
   onion or onion powder
2 tablespoons dried
   oregano
3 tablespoons dried thyme

I recommend grinding this in a coffee grinder to make all pieces equal size. That gives it a better appearance. Store in an airtight container.

World-Famous
Home-Style Mashed Potatoes

I really enjoy mashed potatoes. Not the dressed up kind, but the kind I had growing up as a kid. At Bluephies, we pride ourselves on having really good mashed taters.

4 good-sized baking potatoes (unpeeled), washed, and chopped
1 teaspoon salt
1/2 teaspoon pepper
4 tablespoons butter
1/2 cup cream

Boil the potatoes in a large, uncovered saucepan until they are fork-tender (meaning you can stick a fork into them without resistance). When they are done, drain the water. Place the potatoes in the large bowl of an upright mixer and begin to mash them on low or just break them up with a potato masher. Add salt and pepper. Continue to mix on low or work with a potato masher. Add the butter and cream and mix until they are completely mixed in. The heat from the potatoes will melt the butter.

Leave 'em lumpy.

Makes 3–4 servings.

Zucchini Corn Puffs

This is an adaptable side dish. You can substitute pretty much any kind of vegetable for zucchini.

1/2 cup 2% milk
5 tablespoons butter, cut into pea-sized bites
Pinch of salt
1/4 teaspoon curry powder
Pinch of cayenne pepper
3/4 cup all purpose flour
3 eggs
1/4 pound corn kernels
1/4 pound shredded zucchini
1 1/2 cups grated Parmesan cheese

Preheat oven to 400 degrees.

Bring the milk and butter to a boil in a large saucepan. Add the salt, curry and cayenne pepper. Stir to combine thoroughly. Add the flour all at once and stir to combine. Place back on heat for about 1 minute.

Transfer the mix to an upright mixer. Turn on low speed. When the flour is warm to the touch, add the eggs one at a time. After the eggs are incorporated, add the corn, zucchini, and cheese.

Drop by the spoonful on to a baking sheet. Bake for 15–20 minutes. Or, you can fry them until crispy. This will take about 3–5 minutes.

Makes 4 servings.

A Day in the Life of

6:00 p.m.—Orders for the cooks have been zipping off the kitchen printer, in a steady stream, since 4:30. Everybody's working fast. The breakfast guys left an hour ago after setting up for the next day. The eggs are separated, vegetables chopped, bread for French toast cut, fruit compote checked, and the special scrambler planned. They'll be back to do it all over again at 6:00 a.m. tomorrow. *"Do we have the specials ready?"* **Melanie looks over the menu**—two appetizer specials, a fish special, a lamb special, a pasta special, and three dessert specials. She calls up to the kitchen office on the intercom, **"We have** a lot of reservations, the phone has been ringing nonstop, and there are three big events going on in town. It's going to be a **busy night."**

7:15 p.m. We start to run out of stock on the line. The dinner rush is taking a toll. The sous-chef yells rapid-fire requests to the prep guy for more stock. "I need crab cakes, big tortillas, fettuccini, sushi tuna, and *where is that butternut squash soup I asked for 20 minutes ago?"* Melanie comes back to tell the

line that the 8:00 reservation is for a very regular customer and he's bringing eight people. She asks, "Where is the **chocolate birthday cake** we made to surprise them?" And, she tells me, a customer will call about her dietary restrictions. Someone yells, **"Where's the lobster bisque?"**

8:15 p.m. Four pasta specials, two peppercorn tuna—one rare and one medium—**one calamari appetizer** special, two stuffed salmon salad, three **combo** enchiladas, *Mas pan por favor*.

9:30 p.m. It's starting to slow. The first employee dinner order comes in. The guys on the line talk about what they are going to do after work. We write the supply list for the next day. The prep cook, dishwasher, and bus person start to eat their dinners. *CRASH*—somehow a stack of twenty bread and butter plates **falls to the floor and shatters**.

10:15 p.m. The crew begins taking the stove apart for the nightly cleaning. One guy covers all the open containers of food with plastic wrap and another scrubs the coolers and equipment. Someone turns the radio volume up as diners begin to leave. We discuss the **next day's specials.** Bus tubs full of dirty dishes pile up. Empty squeeze bottles, once filled with olive oil, sauces, and purées, fill the wash tub. Forty minutes later, all the stainless steel surfaces get a last wipe and dirty towels fly into the linen bag.

11:15 p.m. The waitstaff settle their finances. They pay Bluephies the total of their checks; anything more is theirs to keep as tips. Somebody turns the lights up. The anti-fatigue mats that run along the line get scrubbed. The last one to leave **turns the music off and lights out—but it's not over yet.**

12:20 a.m. The nightly cleaning crew shows up. And the lights and radio go back on. Sweeping, mopping, vacuuming, scrubbing and general straightening of the restaurant commences.

4:00 a.m. The cleaners turn the lights out and lock the door. For an hour and 45 minutes **all is quiet**.

5:45 a.m. The back door opens and a blast of **fresh air** races through the restaurant. The first cook of the day flips on the kitchen lights and makes his way to the prep area. He turns on the oven, exhaust fan, and steam table. He slips on his work clothes, grabs an apron and a handful of towels. **Here comes the breakfast stuff**— corned beef hash, jambalaya, eggs Benny, pancake batter, and fruit compote.

6:30 a.m. The second cook shows up and starts to stock the line for the day's business. Breakfast potatoes get sliced and trayed up, eggs cracked—and the list goes on.

8:05 a.m. "**Two eggs easy**, short cakes and a **crab Benny**."
Let the day begin.

Pretty Tasty Black Beans

We use a whole lot of black beans at the restaurant, in many different recipes. We average about 150 pounds of dried black beans a week. This is the first step in getting them out of the bag and into our customers' stomachs.

1 pound black beans, sorted and rinsed
2 quarts water
1/2 cup soy sauce
1 teaspoon vegetable base or 1 bouillon cube

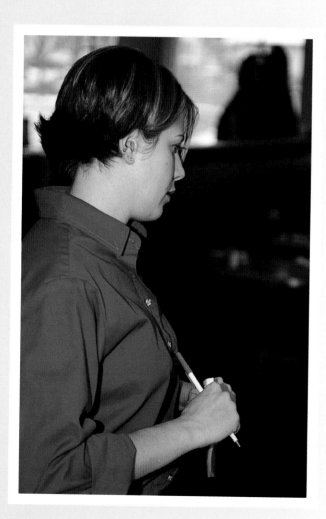

Combine the beans, water, soy sauce, and vegetable base in a medium saucepan; bring to a boil. Reduce the heat and simmer until the liquid is almost all absorbed and evaporated. This will take some time—about 1 1/2 hours, so be patient.

Makes 6 servings.

Black Bean Burgers

We have a lot of items on our menu. We do it by adapting base recipes. Here, we've add a few ingredients to the basic black bean recipe and come up with a lively little burger. At Bluephies, we serve Black Bean Burgers on a toasted bun with lettuce, tomato, and Avocado Ranch Dressing (page 23).

2 cups cooked black beans (page 72)
1 tablespoon chopped fresh cilantro
1 medium red onion, diced
1/2 red pepper, diced
1/2 poblano pepper, diced (green pepper will also work)
1 pinch of black pepper
1/2 teaspoon salt
1 teaspoon minced fresh garlic
1 teaspoon cumin
1/2 teaspoon coriander
1 egg
1 teaspoon puréed chipotle in adobo (available in the Mexican food market or aisle)
1/8 cup cornmeal

Divide the black beans into 2 equal amounts. Add the cilantro, onion, peppers, black pepper, salt, garlic, cumin, and coriander to half the beans; stir to blend.

Put the other half of the beans in a food processor and purée them with the egg and chipotle.

Combine the two mixtures in a large bowl. Fold in the cornmeal to stiffen it a bit and absorb any liquid.

Now make the burgers. Preheat and oil a non-stick sauté pan or a flat-top griddle. Divide the bean mixture into four equal parts. Shape each burger with your hands, until it's about a 1/2-inch thick. Cook for about 5 minutes before flipping. Once the burger's flipped, use the spatula to press it down to the thickness you want.

Makes 4 servings.

Black Bean Corn Relish

This is great in salads, egg scramblers, enchiladas, and sandwiches.

1 cup cooked black beans (page 72)
1 tablespoon chopped cilantro
1/2 medium red onion, diced
1 teaspoon ground ancho chile
1 pinch black pepper
1/2 teaspoon salt
1 teaspoon minced fresh garlic
2 tablespoons olive oil
2 tablespoons lemon juice
1/2 teaspoon cumin
*1 tablespoon red wine
    vinegar*
*1/2 cup corn kernels
    (fresh or frozen)*

Combine the black beans, cilantro, onion, ancho, black pepper, salt, garlic, olive oil, lemon juice, cumin, vinegar, and corn; stir until blended.

Let the mixture sit overnight in the fridge. That's it—you're all set to go.

Makes about 2 cups.

Black Bean Ginger Chipotle BBQ Sauce

This sauce is a great marinade for chicken or pork. We use this sauce for our BBQed Salmon. It has a smoky and sweet taste with a bit of kick. BE CAREFUL when you cook it. It can splash and burn you. It will caramelize, which is good.

1/2 cup sesame oil
1 medium red onion, chopped
1 teaspoon minced fresh garlic
2 teaspoons minced fresh ginger
2 tablespoons puréed chipotle in adobo (available in Mexican food market or aisle)
2 cups orange juice
1/4 cup rice wine vinegar
1 1/2 cups Asian black bean sauce (available in the Asian food market or aisle)
1 tablespoon brown sugar

Heat the sesame oil in a medium-sized saucepan over medium heat. Add the onion and sauté until it starts to caramelize. Add the garlic and ginger; cook for 2–3 minutes. Add the chipotle and cook until it starts to stick a little to the bottom of the saucepan. Add the orange juice, vinegar, black bean sauce, and brown sugar. Bring the sauce to a simmer and reduce the liquid by about 1/3. Purée until smooth.

Makes about 2 1/2 cups.

BRUNCH

Chocolate French Toast

Here's a fun little twist for your brunch. It adds a little spice to the day.

2 eggs
1 tablespoon cocoa
1/4 teaspoon ground cinnamon
1 tablespoon sugar
2 teaspoons ground ancho chile
1/2 cup buttermilk
8 slices sourdough bread, 1 inch thick

Crack the eggs into a large bowl and whisk. Add the cocoa, cinnamon, sugar, and chile. Whisk to blend. Add the buttermilk and stir to mix completely. Try to get all the lumps out.

Dip the sourdough bread into the batter and let it soak for a few minutes. The batter should soak into the bread a little. Don't overdo it or your toast will be pretty pasty when you eat it.

Brush a non-stick griddle or a non-stick pan with butter and lay out your dipped toast.

Cook for about 4 minutes on each side and it is ready to go. Top with some cherry pie filling and chocolate chips—mmmm mmmm GOOD!

Makes enough for 2—in bed, with your dogs at your feet and the paper by your side.

Blueberry Compote

We use a lot of this stuff for topping French Toast (page 80), pancakes, cheesecakes, and Stuffed French Toast (next page). You can also use strawberries or peaches in this recipe.

2 cups frozen blueberries
2 tablespoons sugar
1/4 teaspoon vanilla
1 pinch ground ginger
1 pinch ground cinnamon
1 teaspoon cornstarch
1 tablespoon water

Combine the blueberries, sugar, vanilla, ginger, and cinnamon in a medium saucepan. Heat on low to warm the berries. Mix the cornstarch and water in a separate bowl. When the juice starts to come out of the berries, stir the cornstarch and water mixture into the blueberries. Bring to a full boil. This step is important. It changes the starch and makes the juice thick and clear. If you don't, it will be cloudy and taste starchy.

Makes 2 cups.

Stuffed French Toast

1 cup ricotta cheese
1 cup cream cheese
1 batch Blueberry Compote (page 78)
16 slices cooked French bread, 1 inch thick
1 batch French Toast batter (page 80)
1 tablespoon vegetable oil
Maple syrup

Blend the two cheeses in a food processor or an upright mixer. Add half the fruit compote to the cheese and blend until smooth. Pour the cheese mixture into another bowl and fold in remaining fruit compote. If this filling is too runny, add some panko bread crumbs (Japanese bread crumbs).

Preheat oven to 350 degrees.

Place 8 slices of bread on a baking sheet. Divide the fruit and cheese filling equally on top of the bread slices. Top with the other 8 slices of bread. Heat a griddle or the biggest sauté pan that you own. Dip the stuffed toast into the French Toast dip and place them on the lightly oiled griddle or sauté pan. Cook until golden brown and then gently turn them over. Cook the second side to the same color and then place them back on the baking sheet. Bake in the oven for about 10 minutes to heat all the way through, or pop into your microwave oven for about 1 1/2 minutes. Top with warm maple syrup, more fruit if you like, and serve.

Makes 8 servings.

French Toast

5 eggs
1 tablespoon ground cinnamon
1 teaspoon ground nutmeg
2 tablespoons vanilla
2 cups heavy cream or milk
16 slices sourdough bread, 1 inch thick

To make the batter: Crack the eggs in a large bowl and whisk. Add the cinnamon and nutmeg; whisk to blend. Add the vanilla and cream. Whisk to blend evenly.

Dip the sourdough bread into the batter. The batter should soak into the bread a little. Brush a non-stick pan with butter and lay out your dipped toast. Cook for about 4 minutes on each side.

Makes about 16 pieces of French toast.

Quiche

Quiche is easy. It makes a great little brunch dish and you can add pretty much anything to the basic recipe. Make it even easier on yourself—buy a premade piecrust.

1 9-inch premade piecrust
4 eggs
2 cups heavy cream
2 teaspoons salt
1/2 teaspoon black pepper
1 tablespoon fresh or dried thyme
1 cup filling (see below)

Prebake the crust according to instructions on the wrapper.

Crack the eggs into a medium mixing bowl and whisk them completely. Add the cream, salt, pepper, and thyme. Whisk to blend. That's the basic quiche recipe. Add your choice of filling; stir to mix evenly. You can add spices to complement any filling you use. Pour the mixture into the pie shell. Bake at 375 degrees for 35 to 40 minutes.

Here are some favorite Bluephies fillings. Use a cup of the mixture for each quiche.

Cooked crab, asparagus (steamed briefly), and crumbled feta cheese

or

Pulled roasted chicken (meat separated from the bones) with
*   caramelized onions and mozzarella*

or

Roasted duck with sautéed mushrooms

Makes a 9-inch quiche.

Brunch Bake

Base

8 eggs
1 cup heavy cream
1/2 teaspoon salt
1/4 teaspoon pepper
1/4 teaspoon granulated garlic
8 slices sourdough bread
Filling (see below)
1 cup ground croutons or seasoned bread crumbs

Preheat oven to 350 degrees.

To make the custard mix: Crack the eggs into a large bowl and whisk until blended. Add the cream, salt, pepper, and granulated garlic. Whisk to distribute evenly.

Spray the bottom and sides of a deep-dish pie pan with non-stick spray. Arrange the bread slices on the bottom of the pan and pour half of the custard mix over them.

Fill with a Brunch Bake Filling (see below). Top with the rest of the custard mix. Spread the cheese from the filling mix over the custard. Top with seasoned bread crumbs and bake for 45 minutes.

Makes 6–8 servings.

Filling

Here are my favorite brunch bake fillings. In each case, mix all the ingredients together except the cheese. The cheese goes over the filling.

1 cup diced ham
1 cup sliced mushrooms
1 cup spring peas
1 cup shredded Cheddar cheese

or

1 cup spinach, frozen, thawed (squeezed dry)
1 cup cooked and chopped bacon
1/2 cup medium red onion, minced
1/2 cup minced red pepper
1/2 cup shredded Parmesan cheese

or

1 1/2 cups asparagus, blanched and chopped
1 1/2 cups diced ham
1 cup shredded Swiss cheese

or

1 1/2 cups broccoli, blanched and chopped
1 cup diced ham or cooked chicken
1/2 cup medium red onion, minced
1 cup shredded Cheddar cheese

or

1 cup canned artichoke hearts, chopped
1 cup eggplant, grilled, chopped
1 cup red peppers, roasted, chopped
1 cup mozzarella cheese

or

1 teaspoon of dried dill
1 1/2 cups cooked salmon (smoked is also good)
1 cup asparagus, blanched and chopped
1/2 cup medium red onion, minced
1/2 cup feta cheese

How to Poach Eggs

Don't waste your money buying a fancy egg poacher. You can get perfect poached eggs in five easy steps.

1. Heat 1 quart water with 1 tablespoon white vinegar in a medium-sized saucepan to just below a simmer.

2. Using a large spoon, stir the water in a circle to create a continual and even swirl.

3. Crack up to 6 eggs, one at a time, and drop them gently into the water. As you add each egg, keep it close to the water so you don't get splashed. Drop each egg in towards the center of the swirl. This will keep them separated when you are poaching several eggs.

4. Cook the eggs for about 3 minutes for medium poached, a little longer if you like your eggs harder.

5. Gently scoop out the eggs with a slotted spoon.

Eggs Benedict with Hollandaise Sauce *(page 85),* Crab Cakes *(page 94), and* Crispy Fried Spinach *(page 52)*

Eggs Benedict
with Hollandaise Sauce

We make our hollandaise from scratch—that's the reason it tastes so good. If you make hollandaise sauce the traditional way—by hand with a whisk—your arm muscles will bust out of your shirt. This way is SO easy, with no tired arms.

This is tasty over Eggs Benedict. Sometimes I put roasted artichokes and roasted red peppers on them, sometimes crab cakes and crispy fried spinach.

Hollandaise Sauce
2 egg yolks
1 pinch salt and pepper
1 pinch ground ancho chile
1 teaspoon lemon juice
3/4 cup clarified butter*
1 tablespoon hot water

Blend the egg yolks, salt, pepper, lemon juice, and ground chile in a food processor. With the food processor still running, slowly drizzle in the clarified butter. You must do this slowly or your sauce will separate. Add the water to make the sauce just liquid enough to pour.

Makes enough to cover 4 Benedicts, or about 1 cup.

Eggs Benedict
8 eggs
8 slices Canadian bacon
8 English muffins

Follow the directions for poached eggs (proceeding page). Fry Canadian bacon, and drain on paper towel. Toast muffins.

To assemble: Put two toasted muffins on a plate per serving. Top each with Canadian bacon, 1 poached egg, and hollandaise sauce. That's it.

*To clarify butter, melt the butter, spoon off and discard the white stuff that floats to the top. Pour off the clear butter and discard the stuff that sinks to the bottom.

Billy's Cooking Tips

There's really not much to this cooking business. Anyone with a little intelligence and manual dexterity can become proficient. Some people—like me—really enjoy it. Over the past fifteen years, I've come up with some tips that have made my life in the kitchen easier. So, pay attention.

1. Salt and pepper—use kosher salt and freshly ground pepper. I've found that a seasoning mixture of three parts salt to one part pepper is palatable for most people. Mix 3 tablespoons salt and 1 tablespoon pepper in a small bowl and keep it handy to save time.

2. Use little squeeze bottles for sauté oil. It's convenient and makes your friends think you know what you are doing. You can get these squeeze bottles—like the old-fashioned ketchup and mustard bottles—at any kitchen supply store.

3. When sautéing, little brown caramelized things that stick to your pan are good—they improve flavor. But if they burn and turn black, that's bad. You can't cover up the way burned food tastes.

4. Buy a set of good knives and pans. If you can't afford the whole set, buy a 10-inch chef's knife, and a 10- or 12-inch sauté pan to start. Then build up your collection as you can.

5. Hurry up and get a good, heavy-duty 2- to 3-gallon stockpot. Remember this—thin-bottomed stockpots are only good for boiling water. Your perfect sauces and soups will burn in them easily.

6. Buy the smallest amounts of spices you can. When you run out, go get more. It will take you a long time to go through the really good deal that you found for four jars of thyme and the fifth one free.

7. If you screw up the dish, don't get mad and throw it out. (That's what I do.) Stop and figure out if you can make something out of the part you didn't screw up. Sometimes I've made specials for Bluephies and saved the day, using this practice.

8. Don't buy the new kitchen gadgets that you see on TV. They won't work. Stick with basic knives, spoons, and whisks. They're proven.

9. If you don't marinate the food you are going to cook, season it with salt and pepper. Food by itself tends to be kind of bland.

10. When you grill, keep your grill clean. Brush it with oil, THEN fire it up. Also, add a little extra seasoning to the meat or vegetables. Some seasoning falls off during grilling.

11. Keep in mind that the hot spot on your grill won't cook the food any faster. It'll just burn it.

12. Here's a good tip to successfully sear meat on the grill: Don't move the meat from the heat surface until it will move without sticking.

13. If you're browning meat, actually brown it. Remember, brown is good, black is bad.

14. When smoking food, remember: White smoke is good, black smoke is bad. (Black smoke means you're burning it.)

14. I use panko bread crumbs a lot. They are Japanese-style bread crumbs known for the way they stay crisp. They are lighter and coarser than regular dried bread crumbs. You can find them at Asian markets, specialty stores and sometimes your neighborhood grocery.

MAIN DISHES

All Dressed Up Meat loaf

It's funny how the words "meat loaf" makes you immediately think about the ketchup-topped dish that you had as a kid, and probably still have today. I ran the Bluephies version of meat loaf as a special one night and we sold it so fast, it was dizzying. Today, it is one of our most popular items. I guess our version is kind of a meat loaf in a tuxedo.

1 medium red onion, minced
1 red pepper, minced
1 poblano pepper, minced
1 pound beef tenderloin, cut into bite-sized pieces
1 pound andouille sausage, cut into bite-sized pieces
1 tablespoon minced fresh garlic
1 tablespoon dried thyme
1 teaspoon dried oregano
1 teaspoon black pepper
1 tablespoon salt
6 eggs
1 cup Mae Ploy (Thai sweet chile sauce)
2 1/2 pounds ground beef
3 cups panko bread crumbs (Japanese bread crumbs)

Preheat the oven to 350 degrees.

Put the onion, red pepper, poblano pepper, tenderloin, sausage, garlic, spices, eggs, and Mae Ploy in an upright mixer. Turn on low speed and mix until just combined. Add the ground beef and mix until just combined. Lastly, add the panko and mix to blend. Don't over mix, or the meat loaf will become stringy.

Spray the bottom and sides of a bread loaf pan with non-stick spray and fill it with all of the meat loaf mixture. Spread the meat evenly and then tap the pan on the countertop to eliminate any air pockets that may have formed.

Place the bread pan in a 9 x 13-inch pan. Add water to the 9 x 13-inch pan until it's a quarter full. Cover both pans with foil. Bake for 1 hour and 15 minutes, or until the meat reaches an internal temperature of 160 degrees. Take the temperature of the meat in the center of the meat loaf, as the edges will finish cooking first.

Note: At Bluephies, we let the meat loaf cool, slice it, and then blacken it. To blacken it, pre-heat a cast iron skillet on medium heat. Put a little oil on each slice of the meat loaf. Rub the slice on both sides with Cajun Spices (page 63). Place the slice in the pan and cook for about 3 minutes on each side.

Makes 8 or more servings.

Black Cat Quesadilla

The idea for this dish arrived right out of the blue. When I get tattooed, I bring lunch. One day, the boys at the shop were hungry for beef and guacamole—so, thanks for the inspiration, Black Cat Tattoos.

4 teaspoons vegetable oil
4 flour tortillas (8-inch size)
2 cups shredded Cheddar cheese
1 pound beef tenderloin, marinated in Five-Spice Soy Marinade (page 37),
  cooked, and chopped
2 cups Black Bean Corn Relish (page 74)
8 tablespoons Mae Ploy (Thai sweet chile sauce)
2 cups guacamole
1 cup sour cream
Tortilla Salad (page 16)

Add the oil to the biggest sauté pan you have, and heat it over medium heat. Place the tortilla in the pan and sprinkle the cheese over the entire thing. Add the beef and bean relish to half of the tortilla. Drizzle the Mae Ploy over the meat and beans; fold the tortilla in half. Cook until crisp on one side then flip over and cook until crisp on the other side.

Remove the quesadilla and cut it into three triangles. Lay the triangles on a big plate and divide the guacamole into three equal portions on top of each tortilla. Put equal-sized dollops of sour cream between the tortillas.

To finish the dish like we do at Bluephies, garnish it with a little Tortilla Salad.

Makes 4 servings.

Eggplant Curry Stew

This stew can also be used as a sauce. It could also go over rice, tofu, shrimp, or scallops—you get the idea.

1/4 cup olive oil
1 large yellow onion, diced
5 stalks celery, diced
2 sweet red peppers, chopped
2 pasilla peppers, chopped (green peppers will work)
1 eggplant (unpeeled), chopped
1 1/2 teaspoons minced fresh garlic
1/2 teaspoon minced fresh ginger
1 tablespoon peanut butter
1 teaspoon Chinese Five-Spice Blend (page 55)
1/2 teaspoon cumin
1/2 teaspoon coriander
1 tablespoon curry powder
1 teaspoon salt
1/4 teaspoon black pepper
1/2 teaspoon bottled sriracha hot sauce (Asian food aisle in grocery)
1 can (16 ounces) puréed tomatoes
2 cups water
1 can (14 ounces) coconut milk
1 can (15 ounces) garbanzo beans, drained and rinsed

Heat a large stockpot over medium heat. Add the oil to the pot with onion and celery. Cook, stirring occasionally, until the onion becomes translucent.

Add all the peppers and eggplant. Cook, stirring occasionally, until the eggplant gets soft. Add the garlic, ginger, peanut butter, spices, salt, and pepper. Cook for about 5 more minutes to bring out the flavor.

Add the chile sauce, tomatoes, water, coconut milk, and garbanzos. Simmer until reduced by one quarter.

Makes about 3 quarts, so you have a meal for 6–8 servings of stew, or sauce for a small army.

Chicken Pot Pie

3 tablespoons olive oil
2 pounds boneless, skinless chicken thigh meat, pulled (removed from bones)
1 medium carrot, diced
4 celery stalks, diced
1 large yellow onion, diced
1 tablespoon minced fresh garlic
2 tablespoons soup base (vegetable or chicken)
1 tablespoon dried thyme
2 teaspoons dried oregano
1 teaspoon basil
1 teaspoon dried rubbed sage
1 teaspoon parsley
1 1/2 teaspoons salt
1/4 teaspoon black pepper
1/4 cup flour
4 cups heavy cream
2 cups water
1 large unpeeled russet potato, diced
1 cup corn kernels
2 pastry crusts
1/2 cup shredded Cheddar

There are a couple of ways to make this. One is to use chicken that you have precooked and add it after the vegetables are cooked. The other way is to start with raw chicken and let the chicken shred as it cooks. The latter takes longer, but tastes better.

Heat oil in a heavy stockpot, add the chicken and sauté until it is cooked all the way through. It will begin to shred at this point. Add the carrots, celery, onion, and garlic. Sauté until carrots are tender.

Add the soup base, thyme, oregano, basil, sage, parsley, salt, and pepper. Cook until fragrant.

Add the flour and cook for about 5 minutes, stirring often. Add the cream, water, potatoes, and corn to the pot. Cook until a fork goes through the potatoes without resistance. The starch in the potatoes and the flour will thicken the mixture. If you want a really thick filling, add more flour.

To assemble and bake: Heat oven to 350 degrees.

Put one layer of pastry crust on the bottom of a deep-dish pie pan. Spoon the chicken mixture into the pie dish. Sprinkle the shredded Cheddar over the filling. Cover this with the second sheet of pastry crust. Crimp the edges, cut slits in the crust, and bake until the top crust is golden. Bake at 350 degrees for 45 minutes to an hour until crust is golden and crispy.

Makes 4 servings.

Almond Crust

This is a great breading to use on chicken breasts, or as a topping for Eggplant Curry Stew (page 91).

*1 cup sliced almonds, lightly toasted
    and broken up
1 cup panko (Japanese bread crumbs)
1 cup flour
1 teaspoon salt
1/2 teaspoon dried ground ginger
1/2 teaspoon pepper*

Add all ingredients to a food processor and pulse to blend

Makes enough for 8 chicken breasts.

Crab Cakes

1 cup corn kernels
1 red pepper, diced
1 poblano pepper, diced
1 medium red onion, diced
1 teaspoon minced fresh garlic
1 tablespoon Cajun Spice (page 63)
1 tablespoon olive oil
12 ounces crab meat
2 eggs
1/3 cup Dijon or whole grain mustard
1/2 cup grated Parmesan cheese
1 cup panko bread crumbs (Japanese bread crumbs)
1/4 cup mayonnaise
Vegetable oil to fry

Preheat oven to 350 degrees.

Combine the corn, peppers, onion, garlic, Cajun Spice, and oil in a bowl. Put this mixture in a 9 x 13-inch pan and roast for 10 minutes; let cool.

Drain and squeeze the crabmeat until it's dry. Mix the egg, mustard, cheese, bread crumbs, and mayonnaise together in a large bowl. When the vegetable mixture is cold, add it to the egg mixture and gently fold in the crabmeat so you don't break it up. Divide into 8 equal parts and form them into cakes. Divide into 16 if you're making crab bennies (Benedicts, page 85).

Heat a little oil in a pan, then fry the cakes for 4 minutes each side on medium heat.

Makes 8 cakes.

Euro Scallops

1/2 gallon vegetable oil
1 egg
1 tablespoon water
1/2 cup flour
2 cups croutons, coarsely ground
8 scallops
Salt and pepper

Heat the oil to 350 degrees in a heavy-bottomed saucepan. Check the temperature with your candy thermometer.

Make the egg wash. Crack 1 egg into a bowl. Add 1 tablespoon of water. Whisk to combine.

Sauce for the Euro Scallops

1 tomato
1 red pepper
1/2 large yellow onion
1/4 tablespoon salt
1/4 tablespoon pepper
1/8 cup olive oil
6 cloves garlic
1/4 cup balsamic vinegar
1/8 cup soy sauce
1/8 cup lemon juice

Preheat the oven to 350 degrees.

Toss the tomato, red pepper, onion, garlic, salt, and pepper in oil. Put in a roasting pan and roast for 30 minutes.

Peel the skins off the tomato. Put all the ingredients in a saucepan and simmer until reduced by one-quarter. Cool and purée.

Makes sauce for 4 servings.

While the oil is heating, pat the scallops dry on paper towels. Season them with salt and pepper, and put them in a plastic bag with the flour. Shake them until they are completely covered with flour.

Dip the scallops in the egg wash. Toss them in the ground croutons and fry them in the oil for 1 1/2–2 minutes, depending on their size. Small ones fry quickly and larger ones take longer.

Makes 2 servings.

Mushroom Loaf

This vegetarian "meat loaf" is surprisingly meaty. While developing this dish, we were talking about sauces. "Ketchup," said my sous-chef. All I can say is, "Don't knock it 'til you try it!"

3/4 cup pearl barley
3 cups water
4 tablespoons butter
1 carrot, minced
5 stalks celery, minced
1 large yellow onion, minced
1 tablespoon minced fresh garlic
3 cups minced button mushrooms (Save some time and use the food processor.)
3 portobello mushrooms, sliced
1 tablespoon dried thyme
1 tablespoon dried basil
1 tablespoon dried oregano
2 teaspoons dried rosemary
4 eggs
1/2 cup toasted pecans*
1 cup shredded mozzarella cheese
1 1/2 cups bread crumbs
2 tablespoons Worcestershire sauce
2 tablespoons steak sauce

Toast the barley (with no oil) in a small sauté pan over medium heat. When toasted to a light brown, add the water. Cook until the water is completely soaked into the barley. Keep the barley moving to prevent burning.

Heat the butter in a separate medium-sized sauté pan over medium heat. Add carrots, celery, onion, and garlic. Sauté until the vegetables start to become tender. Add the button and portobello mushrooms. When they begin to release their juices, add the thyme, basil, oregano, and rosemary. Cook until the mushroom liquid has completely evaporated.

When the mushrooms are finished, remove from heat and let the mix cool until you can handle it.

Heat the oven to 350 degrees. Crack the eggs into a large bowl and whisk to blend completely. Add the cooled mushroom mixture, cooked barley, toasted pecans, cheese, bread crumbs, Worcestershire sauce, and steak sauce. Mix by hand to blend.

Spray a bread or pound cake loaf pan with non-stick spray. Place the mushroom mix in the pan. Spread evenly and tap the pan on the counter to make sure there are no air bubbles. Cover the pan with film and foil, then place it in a 9 x 13-inch pan. Fill the bottom pan half full of water. This makes sure it cooks evenly and doesn't burn at the edges. Tapping the loaf will compact it so the slices don't break apart when cut.

Bake for about an hour, or until the temperature of the center of the loaf is 160 degrees.

At Bluephies, we chill the loaf and slice it, grill it, and serve with our World Famous Home-Style Mashed Potatoes (page 64), grilled corn on the cob and, yes, a side of ketchup.

Makes 1 loaf, or about 8 slices

Toast the pecans at 350 degrees for 5 minutes.

Spinach Enchiladas

1 tablespoon olive oil
1 red pepper, diced
1 poblano pepper, diced (green pepper will work, too)
1 medium red onion, diced
1 teaspoon minced fresh garlic
1 teaspoon dried thyme
1 teaspoon dried oregano
1 tablespoon Mae Ploy (Thai sweet chili sauce)—or use your favorite hot sauce
10 ounces fresh spinach (frozen, thawed spinach will work as well)
8 ounces cream cheese
8–10 6-inch flour or corn tortillas
1/2 cup butter
1/2 cup vegetable oil

Heat olive oil in a large pan over a medium flame. Add red pepper, poblano pepper, and onion. Sauté until softened, about 7 minutes.

Add the garlic, thyme, oregano, and Mae Ploy and sauté for a few minutes more. Add the spinach and cook until wilted.

Break up the cream cheese and add it to the pan. Cook until melted and well combined. Keep filling warm.

Makes 8–10 enchiladas.

Rolling & Filling

Heat butter and vegetable oil in a frying pan and stir until blended. Dip each tortilla into the mixture for a couple of seconds. Drain on paper towels.

Put a scoop of filling in the center of the tortilla. Shape the filling into a line, then roll tightly into a log. It's now an enchilada.

Put each enchilada seam-side down on a platter. Repeat until all tortillas are filled and rolled into enchiladas.

Heating

You can:
• bake them in the oven at 350 degrees for 10 minutes; or

• grill them; or

• microwave them on high for 1 1/2 minutes.

Chicken Enchiladas

Mike Seidl, the kitchen manager at Bluephies, is all about enchiladas. These enchiladas have been here for a long time and he has made thousands of them. They are so good they practically stand up on the plate when he is done with them.

8 ounces smoked chicken thighs*
1 cup goat cheese
8 ounces cream cheese, softened
1/2 teaspoon ground cumin
2 tablespoons ground ancho chile
8–10 6-inch flour or corn tortillas

Chop or shred the chicken thigh meat. Blend the goat cheese, cream cheese, cumin, and chile in an upright mixer or food processor. Once combined, add the chicken, but don't run the food processor much longer. Make sure you still have noticeable bits of chicken.

See previous page for enchilada rolling and baking directions.

Makes 8-10 enchiladas.

*BIG NOTE: We smoke the chicken to add more flavor. To smoke meat, soak wood chips in water for about 30 minutes. Meanwhile, heat coals in an outdoor grill. Poke holes in a disposable pie pan. Put the chips in the pan and the pan directly on the hot coals. (Or, put the damp wood chips right on the hot coals and the chicken on the grill rack.)

Put the chicken on a rack over the coals, cover the grill and cook the chicken until done. That will depend on how hot the coals are. Remember, the longer the meat stays in smoke, the more flavor it gains. You can also rub cumin and chile on the meat before you smoke it, for more flavor. I like to use thighs for this because they stay moist and have a meatier flavor.

Herb Roasted Chicken

Sunday night at Bluephies is a good time. All the weekend hoopla is winding down. A simple meal is exactly what I want. So we created the "Sunday Night Supper"— a family-style meal with fresh-baked apple pie. The main attraction is my Herb Roasted Chicken. Plan ahead for this one because you'll have to marinate the chicken.

1 whole chicken, 5–7 pounds
1/4 cup whole-grain or Dijon mustard
1 tablespoon minced fresh garlic
2 tablespoons olive oil
1 teaspoon black pepper
1/4 teaspoon fresh rosemary
1 teaspoon dried oregano
1 teaspoon dried thyme
1 lemon

Note: If you use fresh herbs, double the amount of herbs because the one-two punch of marinating and roasting will decrease their strength.

Wash the chicken and dry it with a towel to remove the extra moisture. Mix the mustard, garlic, oil, spices, and the juice of the lemon in a large bowl. Save the squeezed lemon rind.

Add the chicken to the mustard mixture. Rub the mixture on both the inside and outside of the chicken. Put the rind of the squeezed lemon in the cavity of the chicken. Let it marinate overnight in the fridge. At Bluephies, I let chickens sit for two days.

Preheat oven to 425 degrees.

Remove the chicken from the marinade and place the chicken on a roasting rack in a pan. Cook in the oven for 15 minutes to give the skin a golden color and make it crispy.

Lower the heat to 350 degrees and cook until the chicken reaches an internal temperature—in the thigh area—of 160 degrees; about 10 minutes per pound is a good rule. Save the drippings for gravy.* Remove the lemon before you cut and serve the chicken.

Use leftovers in Chicken Apple Walnut Salad (page 19).

Makes 1 really awesome chicken.

*To make gravy, heat pan drippings and thicken with 2 tablespoons flour. Stir in 2 cups of cream. Add salt and pepper to taste.

Lamb Shank Redemption
(or Silence 'Em with Lamb Shanks)

This is the ultimate in comfort food. Serve it up over Home-Style Mashed Potatoes (page 64) or Yummy Polenta (page 56).

2 lamb shanks
Salt and pepper to season the shanks
Seasoned Flour (page 106)
1/2 cup olive oil
1 small carrot, diced
1 stalks celery, diced
1/2 large yellow onion, diced
2 cups chopped wild mushrooms (or any mushrooms will work)
1 tablespoon minced fresh garlic
1 teaspoon dried thyme
1 teaspoon dried oregano
1 teaspoon rosemary
1/2 cup white wine
2 tomatoes, cored and quartered
1 cup stock (beef, chicken, vegetable, or veal will work)

Preheat oven to 325 degrees.

Season the lamb and vegetables with salt and pepper. Then dredge the meat in the seasoned flour.

Pour the oil into a 10-inch heavy-bottomed ovenproof stockpot and heat over medium heat on your stovetop. Add the lamb shanks to the pan and brown the meat. The flour should cook to a hard and golden crust. Don't move the meat until the crust has formed. It makes it look pretty. Turn the meat over and brown the other side.

Add the carrots, celery, and onion to the pot and sauté until soft. Add the mushrooms and garlic. Cook until the mushrooms are starting to seep their liquid. The garlic will be tender at this point as well.

Add the thyme, oregano, and rosemary. Sauté until fragrant—about 5 minutes. Add the wine and deglaze the pan (scrape the sides and bottom and stir to make a sauce.). Bring the wine up to a simmer. Add the tomatoes and stock. Remove from heat.

Cover the top of the pan with an ovenproof top or a big piece of aluminum foil. Use oven mitts. Put it in the oven and cook for 2 hours.

Makes 2 servings plus sauce for the meat.

Root Vegetable Ragout

There are a lot of ingredients in this recipe, but if you cook it slowly and stir it occasionally, this ragout will do all the work for you. You can use pretty much any root vegetable for this recipe. Here's what we use in the restaurant.

1 turnip, peeled and cubed
1 celery root, cleaned and cubed
1 rutabaga, peeled and cubed
1 sweet potato, peeled and cubed
1 carrot, peeled and cubed
2 red peppers, chopped
1 large yellow onion, chopped
3 tablespoons olive oil, divided
1 sprig fresh rosemary
1 teaspoon salt
1 pinch black pepper
1 teaspoon dried thyme
1 teaspoon dried oregano
1 tablespoon minced fresh garlic
1 1/2 cups white wine (this might seem like a lot, but I like the fruitiness it
*   gives the dish)*
2 cups heavy cream

Preheat oven to 350 degrees.

Combine half each of the turnip, celery root, rutabaga, sweet potato, carrot, red pepper, and onion in a bowl. Toss with 1 tablespoon of olive oil, the sprig of rosemary, salt, and pepper. Once the vegetables are completely coated with oil and spices, put this mixture in a 9 x 13-inch pan. Roast the vegetables in the oven for about 25 minutes or until the vegetables are slightly browned. Don't be alarmed when you see how much the vegetables shrink.

While half the vegetables are roasting, sauté the other half in the remaining olive oil in either a heavy-bottomed stockpot or a sauté pan over medium heat. They might stick to the bottom of the pot—just stir them and they will be okay. Add the thyme, oregano, and garlic. The pan will develop some caramelized spots where the vegetables are resting. That's good; it adds flavor, as long as you don't burn them.

After about 8 minutes, add the white wine and deglaze the pan (scrape the sides and bottom of the pan and stir to make a sauce.) This is where the flavor develops. Continue cooking until the wine is reduced by one fourth, then add the cream.

Cook until the vegetables are tender and the cream is thickened from the natural starches in the vegetables.

Once the oven-roasted vegetables are done, combine them with the sautéed vegetables. Stir them all together and call it done.

This is REALLY good over polenta (page 56) with fresh Parmesan cheese.

Makes 6 servings.

Rotollo

My wife, Melanie, loves butternut squash. She also is crazy about goat cheese. This combination of the two, rolled up in pasta, is so sweet, cheesy, and good that it ended up on our fall and winter menu. Put a sauce of your choosing over these and you will be amazed. Pick one from the Marinades and Sauces section starting on page 28.

2 butternut squash, roasted, skins removed, flesh puréed
1 teaspoon dried thyme
1 teaspoon dried oregano
1/4 teaspoon dried rubbed sage
1 teaspoon salt
1/4 teaspoon black pepper
1/2 cup goat cheese
4 lasagna sheets, prepared according to directions on the box (use dried
lasagna sheets, or precooked sheets)

Preheat the oven to 350 degrees.

Blend the puréed squash, thyme, oregano, sage, salt, pepper, and goat cheese in an upright mixer with a paddle attachment, on low speed.

Divide the squash mix into 4 equal parts and spread it out over the sheets of cooked pasta. Roll up the pasta gently. Don't roll it too tight or your filling will squeeze out.

Bake covered for about 20 minutes with a little water in the pan.

Makes 4 large rolls.

Spinach-Stuffed Trout

I like to use this filling to stuff rainbow trout. It also works well for topping baked or grilled oysters.

1/2 pound (2 sticks) butter
1 large yellow onion, diced
1 tablespoon minced fresh garlic
2 pinches dried thyme
8 ounces fresh baby spinach, chopped
1/4 cup lemon juice
5 dashes Tabasco sauce
1 teaspoon salt
Pinch of black pepper
1/4 cup grated Parmesan
2 cups panko bread crumbs (Japanese bread crumbs)
6-8 trout, boneless, headless

Melt the butter in a large saucepan over medium flame. Add the onion, garlic, and thyme and cook until the onion is translucent.

Add the spinach and cook until wilted (just a few minutes—don't lose the bright green color). Add the lemon juice, Tabasco, salt and pepper. While the mixture is still hot, add the cheese and bread crumbs, and stir to combine.

Stuff the fish. I like to get boneless, headless trout so they are ready to go. The extra cost is well worth it. Put the fish skin side down on a work surface and dry the flesh with a paper towel. Season it with a little salt and pepper and then place the filling in the center of the fish—right down the middle. Be careful not to use too much filling. If you do, the fish will dry out before the filling is hot. Fold the fish so it has the approximate shape it did when it was still swimming around. Dry the outside of the fish with a paper towel and add a little olive oil, salt and pepper to the skin.

You can either grill or fry the trout in more olive oil or butter. When it's cooked a bit, place it in an ovenproof pan, top with lemon slices, and bake it for about 12 minutes at 350 degrees. Push on the fish to see if it's done. It should be firm and resistant but there shouldn't be an imprint where you touched it. Cook it through. Undercooked trout is not good.

Makes about 3 cups of filling and about 6-8 servings of trout.

Thai Peanut Chicken

Here is a simple but good pasta to make with leftovers from some of our other recipes. It's how we come up with many of our specials and menu items. Borrowing a part of one dish and incorporating it into another can give a completely different result. If the two parts are good to begin with, then they will either complement or contrast and BINGO—you've got a new dish.

2 tablespoons vegetable oil
1 small handful toasted, unsalted peanuts*
1 cooked chicken breast, diced or pulled
2 cups Asian Slaw (page 20)
4 tablespoons hoisin sauce (Asian sweet-sour, slightly spicy sauce)
4 ounces bottled Mae Ploy (Thai sweet chile sauce)
6 ounces cooked rice or bean thread noodles (follow directions on package
    for cooking)

Add the oil to a large sauté pan over medium heat. Toss in the peanuts and cook them so they turn slightly brown. If you're afraid you might burn them, add them at the end of the dish.

Toss the chicken into the pan and just warm it through. Then add the Asian Slaw and cook until greens are wilted. Add the hoisin and Mae Ploy. Now, let this cook a little and bring out the flavors. Add your noodles and heat through.

TA-DA! You got a fast, really good meal with no sweat. I should have my own cooking show!

Makes 2 servings.

*Toast peanuts at 350 degrees for 5 minutes.

Seasoned Flour

This is an all-purpose seasoning flour. Coat meat with it before browning.

1/4 cup all purpose flour
1/2 teaspoon salt
1/3 teaspoon black pepper
1/4 teaspoon celery salt

Combine all ingredients in a small mixing bowl and mix thoroughly. Then pour mixture in a bag, drop the meat in and shake to coat.

Makes enough flour to coat 4 lamb shanks, 6 chicken breasts, or 4 pork or veal cutlets.

Sweet Potato & Chorizo Au Gratin

This is my idea of "retro chic" scalloped potatoes and ham. I remember the familiar smells of milk, ham, potatoes, and cheese when Mom made it. This is a nod to the old with the look and flavor of today.

3 medium sweet potatoes, peeled and sliced as thinly as possible
12 ounces cooked chorizo*
3 cups shredded smoked mozzarella
4 eggs
1/2 cup heavy cream
1 tablespoon dried oregano
1 tablespoon dried thyme
3 tablespoons puréed chipotle in adobo

Preheat the oven to 350 degrees.

Spray the bottom and sides of a 9 x 13-inch pan with non-stick spray. Lay the sliced sweet potatoes, slightly overlapping, along the bottom of the pan.

Spread a quarter of the cooked chorizo on top of the potatoes. To that, add a quarter of the shredded cheese. Repeat this process until the chorizo and cheese are all used up. For best results, the gratin should be four layers tall.

Mix the eggs, cream, and spices together in a small mixing bowl. Blend and pour over the entire mixture. Cover the entire pan with plastic film, then cover completely with aluminum foil. Bake until the potatoes are tender and the center of the dish is firm to the touch, about 1 hour and 15 minutes.

Tips: For professional results, alternate the direction of your potatoes when layering them (one layer length-wise, one layer width-wise). This will give the gratin more strength to stand up when you cut it. Also, let the dish cool a little before serving, so it sets up.

Makes a 9 x 13-inch pan, 12 servings.

*Use Mexican-style chorizo; it breaks up like hamburger when it cools. (Spanish chorizo is a garlicky cured sausage—not the same thing at all.)

Vegetable Strudel

A long time ago, vegetarian food consisted of steamed vegetables and some noodles with cream sauce. Those days are over. Here is a really popular dish with our vegetarian customers at Bluephies.

1 red pepper, sliced thin
2 medium red onions, sliced thin
2 yellow squash, cut into spaghetti-sized strands
2 zucchini, cut into spaghetti-sized strands
2 tablespoons olive oil
1 tablespoon salt
1 teaspoon black pepper
2 teaspoons dried thyme
1 teaspoon dried oregano
1/4 cup chopped kalamata olives
1 16-ounce package thawed phyllo dough
1/2 pound clarified butter*
1/4 cup dried parsley
24 blanched asparagus spears

Combine the peppers, onions, yellow squash, and zucchini in a large mixing bowl. Toss them with the oil, salt, pepper, thyme, and oregano.

Heat a large sauté pan on high heat until hot. Drop in the vegetables all at once. You want a thin layer of vegetables so that you sear all of them. Do it in batches if necessary. When the vegetables are all seared, add the olives and remove from heat

Divide the vegetables into six equal parts. Unfold the phyllo dough and place a barely damp towel over the dough to keep it moist. Take a piece of parchment paper and place on a level surface (like your counter top). Put one piece of phyllo dough on the paper and brush the dough with butter, working from the outside edge in. Sprinkle some of the dried parsley on top of the first sheet and then cover with another sheet of phyllo. Brush with butter and add another piece of phyllo. Brush again with butter and cover with another piece of phyllo. That is your base for the strudel.

Take 1 of the 6 parts of the vegetable mix. Spread it out on the side of the dough near you. Place 4 spears of asparagus on top of the vegetables.

Now you roll it. Take the edge of the parchment that is close to you, where the vegetables are, and slowly roll the dough over the vegetables using the parchment to help. Tuck the dough in and make the roll as tight as you can.

Peel back the parchment and brush butter on the rolled part. Slowly and tightly roll the remaining phyllo, taking care to brush butter on as you expose unbuttered dough. This is important because it makes the dough stick to itself and it stays together while it's cooking.

Do this until all the dough is gone. I get about 6 rolls per batch.

To bake, spray a cookie sheet with non-stick spray and cut the strudel at angles, so the pieces are about 2 inches tall. Stand them up on the tray and bake at 350 degrees until golden brown.

Makes 6 rolls, and you can cut into as many servings as you like.

* To clarify butter, melt the butter, spoon off and discard the white stuff that floats to the top. Pour off the clear butter and discard the stuff that sinks to the bottom. (Or put it in the dog's dish. He'll be thrilled.)

Vegetable Strudel *on mixed greens with* Lemon Vinaigrette *(page 24)*

DESSERTS

Evil Snickers Pie

It must be the kid in me, but I like candy. So, I make some pretty tall pies that are all about sugar highs. Note: You can use a premade crust or make your own. Either way, get ready to call your dentist.

This one contains Snickers, but I have also been accused of substituting M&Ms, Butterfingers, or Oreos.

If you can't find crushed candy, just freeze the ones you want to use and grind them up in a food processor, but be sure to break the bars into smaller pieces first.

1 pound cream cheese, at room temperature
4 tablespoons butter
1/3 cup sugar
1 teaspoon vanilla extract
1 cup crushed Snickers
1 nine-inch pie shell, baked (Try the Incredible Chocolate Crust, page 121)

Mix the cream cheese, butter, sugar, and vanilla in an upright mixer on low speed until blended. Turn to high speed once it's blended to make it nice and fluffy.

Add 2/3 cup of the Snickers and mix until just blended through. Scoop out the mix into the baked pie shell. Use your hands to spread it out (afterward, you can lick your fingers). Sprinkle the remaining Snickers over the top.

Makes 1 HUGE 9-inch pie.

(Left) "Pie by Night"

Lemon or Lime Pie

This is really simple. All you need is five minutes to make it and one hour to bake it. The process to make a lemon or lime pie is basically the same. The ingredients are slightly different. Top off with whipped cream.

Lemon Pie Filling

2 whole eggs
4 eggs yolks
2 14-ounce cans sweetened condensed milk
Zest and juice of 3 lemons*
1 nine-inch pie shell, baked

or

Lime Pie Filling

2 whole eggs
4 egg yolks
2 14-ounce cans sweetened condensed milk
1 cup bottled Key lime juice
1 nine-inch graham cracker crust pie shell

Preheat oven to 350 degrees.

Crack the whole eggs into a large bowl. In another bowl, separate the remaining egg whites and egg yolks. Add the egg yolks to the whole eggs. Whisk to combine.

Add the sweetened condensed milk and whisk to blend. Add the lemon zest and juice (or lime juice). Stir to combine.

Pour the mixture into the pie shell. Bake for 1 hour. Cool in the refrigerator. Top with whipped cream and—**wham-bam**—it's done.

Makes 6–8 servings.

Whipped Cream

Throw out your frozen whipped topping. Look how easy this is.

2 cups cold heavy cream
1/2 cup sugar

Add the cream and sugar to a cold, upright mixing bowl. Turn the mixer on high and let it whip. In less than 5 minutes, your cream will hold stiff peaks and it's ready to spread on a lower crust CHILLED pie.

Topping for a 9-inch pie.

*To zest, grate the yellow peel of the lemon with a fine grater. Don't grate the white pith; it's bitter.

Almond Tuille Cookies

These crunchy little things are so addictive. You won't be able to stop at just one.

1 pound (4 sticks) unsalted butter
3 cups sugar
10 egg whites
1 tablespoon vanilla extract
1 1/4 cups flour
1 teaspoon salt
4 cups sliced almonds

Preheat the oven to 350 degrees. Line a baking sheet with parchment paper.

Blend the butter and sugar in an upright mixer until light and fluffy. Add the egg whites and vanilla; mix to combine. Sift the flour and salt together and add this to the bowl. Mix thoroughly. Lastly, mix in the almonds until incorporated.

Scoop the dough in 2-ounce scoops onto the lined baking sheet. Bake 10 minutes. Spin the cookie sheet around and cook for 10 minutes more. They should be done at this point. If not, bake them until the cookies are golden brown on the edges only. They will be thin and crispy.

The dough freezes well, but let it thaw before you bake.

Makes about 24 cookies.

Cherry Pie Filling

Melanie, my wife, loves this pie filling. It has the perfect blend of tartness and sweetness—kind of like her. This filling is for the inside of the Chocolate Chile Bread Pudding (page 115). Once you make this filling, you will NEVER buy canned filling again.

2 pounds cherries, frozen
1 cup sugar
1 tablespoon brandy
1/2 teaspoon almond extract
4 tablespoons cornstarch
6 tablespoons water

This is a simple process. Follow the directions and don't think about what you are doing.

Combine the cherries and sugar in a medium saucepan and cook over medium heat until they have released their liquid. You will be surprised by how much liquid they release.

Pour the cherries into a strainer that has been placed inside a large bowl to catch the juice. Once all of the juice is drained, pour the liquid back into the saucepan. To this, add the brandy and the almond extract. Whisk the cornstarch into the cherry juice and bring to a boil. This is the BIG important part! If you don't bring this to a boil, this pie filling won't thicken right and the filling will be cloudy. Once the juice has thickened to a paste consistency, add the water, and add the cherries back into the juice. Fold to combine.

It's that simple, but man is it good.

Makes enough for a 9-inch pie, or a whole bunch of bread puddings.

Chocolate Chile Bread Pudding

Add a little spice to your dessert. This will put a tingle in the back of your mouth.

8 ounces bittersweet chocolate, chopped
4 cups chopped crusty white bread
1 1/3 cups heavy cream
2 tablespoons + 2 teaspoons sugar
1 tablespoon vanilla extract
1 teaspoon cinnamon
2 teaspoons ground ancho chile or your favorite ground chiles (no seeds)
4 eggs, beaten
4 tablespoons Cherry Pie Filling (page 114)

Preheat oven to 350 degrees.

Put the chocolate in a mixing bowl. Put the chopped white bread in a separate large mixing bowl.

Combine cream and sugar in a small saucepan on medium heat; bring to a boil. Pour the boiling liquid over the chocolate in the mixing bowl. Stir to melt the chocolate. Once melted, add the vanilla, cinnamon, and chile.

Pour this mixture over the chopped bread in the large mixing bowl. Stir in the egg and let it stand for about 10 minutes.

Spray 4 1-cup ovenproof ramekins with non-stick spray. Scoop one-quarter of the bread mixture into each and put on a layer of the Cherry Pie Filling. Top with the remaining bread mixture. Bake at 350 degrees for 10–15 minutes. Serve warm.

Makes 4 servings.

Brown Sugar Vanilla Crème Brûlée

This dessert has been on our menu forever. We have tried other variations but we always come back to this one.

2 egg yolks
1 cup heavy cream
3 tablespoons brown sugar
2 teaspoons vanilla extract
Additional sugar

Preheat oven to 350 degrees.

Place the egg yolks in a small bowl and whisk until smooth. Bring the cream, sugar, and vanilla to a boil in a small saucepan, making sure to dissolve the sugar. Slowly pour the hot cream mixture over the egg yolks, whisking as you go. Pour it in slowly or you will end up with really sweet scrambled eggs.

Pour the custard mix into shallow coffee cups (cappuccino cups work well). Place them in an ovenproof pan. Fill the pan half-full with water. Bake until the custard is almost set up, about 1 hour.

Remove from oven and let them cool for 15 minutes, then place in the refrigerator to cool completely. Don't put them in the freezer; they must cool slowly and completely to be good.

To finish the dessert, sprinkle a thin, even layer of sugar across the top and caramelize in the broiler or with a torch.

Makes 1 big or 2 average-size desserts. This recipe can be doubled to make 2–4 servings.

Chocolate Raspberry Crème Brûlée

2 egg yolks
1 cup heavy cream
1 tablespoon sugar
1 tablespoon raspberry sauce
2 tablespoons semisweet chocolate chips
Additional sugar

Preheat oven to 350 degrees.

Place the egg yolks in a small bowl and whisk until smooth. Bring the cream, sugar and raspberry sauce to a boil in a small saucepan; make sure you dissolve the sugar. Slowly pour the hot cream mixture over the egg yolks, whisking to combine. Pour it slowly or you will end up with chocolate-raspberry scrambled eggs.

Pour the custard mix into shallow coffee cups (cappuccino cups work well). Place them in an ovenproof pan. Fill the pan half-full of water and bake until the custard is almost set up, about 1 hour.

Remove from oven and let cool for 15 minutes at room temperature. Then place them in the refrigerator to cool completely. Don't put them in the freezer; they must cool slowly and completely to be good.

To finish the dessert, sprinkle a thin, even layer of sugar across the top and caramelize in the broiler or with a torch.

Makes 1 big or 2 average-size desserts. This recipe can be doubled to make 2–4 servings.

Butterfinger Wontons

These little guys are a lot of fun to make. This recipe is one of my food reinvention ideas.

If you can't find a crushed version of Butterfingers in the baking aisle, freeze some and grind them in a food processor. Break them into smaller pieces before you work them over in the food processor.

4 ounces cream cheese, at room temperature
1/8 cup sugar
1/4 teaspoon vanilla extract
2 tablespoons butter, at room temperature
1/4 cup crushed Butterfingers
24 wonton wrappers, thawed
1/3 gallon vegetable oil

Blend the cream cheese, sugar, vanilla, and butter in an upright mixer on low speed. Once mixed, turn up to high speed to make it fluffy. Stir in the Butterfingers until just mixed through.

Follow the directions on the next page for filling and wrapping a wonton. Then freeze the wontons for best results. (They'll hold together better when you fry them.)

Heat the vegetable oil to 350 degrees, and fry the wontons in batches for about 1 1/2 minutes. We serve them with vanilla ice cream.

Makes 4 servings. Double this recipe for 8 servings.

How to Fold a Wonton

1. Put dab of filling in center of the wonton wrap.

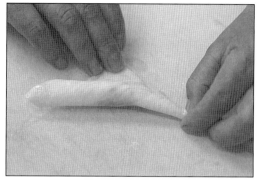

2. Fold the wrap diagonally in half to form a triangle.

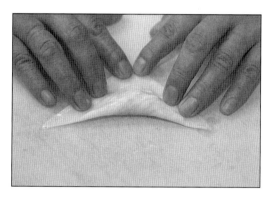

3. Crimp the edges to seal in filling.

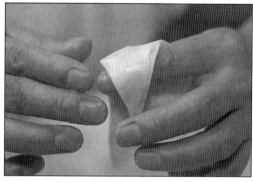

4. Moisten lightly, then wrap outside point around finger.

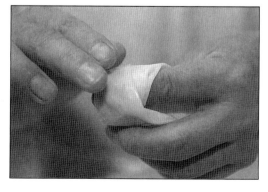

5. Wrap opposite point around finger and crimp ends together.

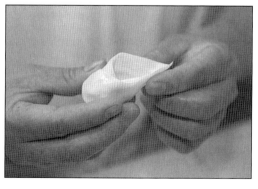

6. Pinch wonton together to flatten a bit.

Chocolate Toffee Coffee Cheesecake

You will need a big upright mixer for this one.

4 ounces bittersweet chocolate
8 ounces semisweet chocolate
2 pounds cream cheese, at room temperature
3/4 cup sugar
1 teaspoon vanilla
1 cup coffee-flavored liqueur
4 eggs
Incredible Chocolate Crust (next page)
Ganache (page 122)
1/2 recipe Hard Toffee (page 123)

Heat oven to 350 degrees.

Melt the chocolates together in a double boiler—melting them in the microwave will work, too.

Place the cream cheese, sugar and vanilla in a mixer. Using the paddle attachment, blend on low speed and keep it there. You don't want to incorporate air. Blend until the mixture is completely smooth.

Add coffee liqueur to the mix and blend through. Add the melted chocolate to the mixer. Make sure to scrape down the sides of the bowl. Add the eggs and blend to combine.

Pour this out into the cooked chocolate crust and bake for about 1 hour, then jiggle it. It's done when it's still a little jiggly in the center. (It will continue to cook for a little bit after you remove it from the oven.) Leave it in the mold to cool, and let it cool to room temperature before you refrigerate it.

To finish: unmold the cheesecake. Top with Ganache. Break up the Hard Toffee and place one generous piece on each serving.

Makes 1 incredible cheesecake, about 10–14 servings.

Incredible Chocolate Crust

We use this crust for a few of our desserts. It was created for the Chocolate Toffee Coffee Cheesecake (previous page).

1/4 pound (1 stick) butter
1/2 cup sugar
1/4 teaspoon vanilla extract
1 good-size tablespoon cocoa
2/3 cup flour

Preheat oven to 350 degrees.

Combine all of the ingredients in an upright mixer. Using the paddle attachment, mix on low speed until it forms a thick dough and clings to the paddle.

Spread mixture on the bottom of an 8- or 9-inch springform pan and bake for 25 minutes. The crust will bubble and look wet when it comes out of the oven, so be careful to keep it flat—don't tilt it. When it cools, the crust will get crisp.

Makes an 8- or 9-inch crust.

Ganache

Ganache—pronounced ga-Nosh—a sweet creamy chocolate mixture used especially as a filling or frosting.

Use good quality chocolate. The extra money you spend to get a better product will be well rewarded. This recipe is used to top our Chocolate Toffee Coffee Cheesecake (page 120).

1 cup semisweet chocolate (chopped bars or chips)
1 tablespoon light corn syrup
1/2 cup whipping cream

Place semisweet chocolate and corn syrup in a mixing bowl and set aside.

Heat the cream in a saucepan. Bring to a boil and pour it over the chocolate. Stir the mixture until it's smooth and the chocolate is completely melted. If the chocolate is not fully melted, finish melting over a double boiler.

This will keep refrigerated up to one week, but you can use it on so many desserts that it won't last that long!

To reheat, use a double boiler.

Makes enough to top an 8-inch cheesecake.

Chocolate Toffee Coffee Cheesecake *(page 120) drizzled with chocolate and caramel topping and* Whipped Cream *(page 112)*

Hard Toffee

We use this as part of the topping for the Chocolate Toffee Coffee Cheesecake (page 120).

You will need a candy thermometer for this recipe.

Be careful when you are making it. Hot sugar really hurts if it gets on you. Also, use oven mitts when you are moving your cookie sheet.

1/2 pound (2 sticks) butter
1 cup sugar
1 tablespoon light corn syrup
1/2 cup chopped pecans

Heat the butter, sugar, and corn syrup in a small saucepan over medium heat, until the temperature reaches 300 degrees.

Remove the saucepan from heat and stir in the pecans. Place a piece of parchment paper on a cookie sheet and pour the hot toffee onto it. Use an offset spatula—a frosting spreader—and spread the toffee as thinly as you can. Try to make a continuous sheet of toffee, no more than 1/4-inch thick.

Cool toffee in the refrigerator. Break off the size of pieces you want for your cheesecake. Or, eat the toffee by itself for a quick little snack. Add it to ice cream. YUM!

Makes enough for 2 cheesecakes.

Flourless Chocolate Cake

Jake Gundy, my first sous-chef, created this cake for me back in 2001. It has been on our menu ever since. A little slice will make anyone happy—and it freezes well.

1/2 cup plus 2 tablespoons brewed coffee
Scant 3/4 cup sugar
10 ounces bittersweet chocolate
10 tablespoons butter, melted
5 egg yolks, whisked until smooth
Powdered cocoa or chocolate sauce

Preheat oven to 350 degrees.

Heat the coffee and sugar in a medium saucepan until the coffee comes to a boil and the sugar dissolves.

Put the chocolate in a heat-proof mixing bowl. Pour the boiling coffee over the chocolate and stir until the chocolate is completely melted. Add the melted butter to the chocolate. Stir to combine.

Add the whisked egg yolks to the chocolate mixture. Stir to combine. Let cool so it sets up (thickens a little).

Spray a springform (cheesecake) pan with nonstick spray. Scrape all the filling into the pan. Bake 35–45 minutes. When the cake is done, the top won't jiggle and a crust will have just begun to form.

Cool completely. To unmold, run a wet, hot knife under the cake to loosen it from the bottom of the form.

You can use more filling to make a bigger cake, but you'll need to increase the cooking time. You can also substitute semisweet chocolate for the bittersweet, but if you do, omit the sugar.

Dust the cake with cocoa, or drizzle with chocolate sauce before serving.

Makes 1 cake, 8–12 servings.

Carrot Cake

We serve seven carrot cakes to customers every week. That's impressive considering each is actually six layers of cake. Add in six layers of rich cream cheese frosting and our cake tips the scale at about eighteen pounds of moist, creamy goodness. This version is smaller, enough for two layers.

3/4 cup vegetable oil
2 eggs, beaten
1 1/8 teaspoons vanilla extract
1 1/2 cups sugar
1 1/2 cups flour
1/2 teaspoon salt
1 1/4 teaspoons cinnamon
1 1/4 teaspoons baking soda
3/4 cup shredded coconut
1 1/2 cups shredded carrots
1/2 cup crushed pineapple
Cream Cheese Frosting

Preheat oven to 350 degrees. Spray a 10-inch cake pan with non-stick spray. Place a round piece of parchment paper in the bottom of the cake pan.

Mix the oil, eggs, and vanilla on low speed in an upright mixer until well blended. Slowly add the sugar, flour, salt, cinnamon, and baking soda while the mixer is running. Lastly, add the coconut, carrots, and pineapple until just incorporated. Spread mixture in prepared pan. Bake for one hour. Stick a toothpick in the center. If it comes out clean, it's done. If not, continue baking and check at 5-minute intervals until done.

Cool the cake. Cut into two layers and frost with

Cream Cheese Frosting
Easy as 1-2-3!

8 ounces cream cheese, room temperature
1/4 pound butter (1 stick)
1 cup powdered sugar

Blend the butter and cream cheese on low speed to eliminate any lumps in the frosting. Then add the sugar and continue to blend on low speed until smooth.

Makes one 10-inch round cake, enough for 10–14 servings.

Cream Puffs

There's nothing like cream puffs for that great combination of chewy texture and sweetness. Just try to eat less than three of these things.

Puffs

1 cup water + 1 tablespoon
2 teaspoons sugar
8 tablespoons butter (1 stick)
1/2 teaspoon salt
1 cup flour
1 egg + 4 eggs

Heat oven to 425 degrees.

Make the egg wash. Crack 1 egg into a bowl. Add 1 tablespoon water. Whisk to combine.

Boil the water, sugar, butter, and salt together. Remove from heat. Add all the flour and stir to incorporate. Return to the heat for 45 seconds so the flour cooks a bit.

Put the dough in an upright mixer with a paddle and mix on low. Blend until the dough reaches room temperature, and then add the eggs, one at a time. Scrape down the sides of the bowl. Add each successive egg after the previous one is completely incorporated. The dough should pull away from the paddle.

Plop a scoop of dough about an inch and a half in diameter onto a baking sheet lined with parchment paper, and brush with a little egg wash. Bake for 15 minutes, then reduce the temperature to 375 degrees and bake for 25 more minutes. Don't open the door until it's done. Take the sheet out and let it cool completely.

Filling

Use ice cream or Cream Cheese Frosting (page 125)

Cut cream puffs in half horizontally and place a scoop of ice cream between the halves. You can also put cream cheese in a pastry bag and pipe it into the center of the puff. Top with chocolate or caramel sauce.

Makes about 20 puffs.

All sorts of folks love to devour Billy's Cream Puffs.

Down Home Fruit Crisp

I've got a thing for pies and crisps. What can I say? The smell of a pie or crisp baking is one of the simple pleasures of life. Over-the-top desserts are great, but don't forget the simple ones. Here is my "Ode to the Simple Stuff."

Topping

This adaptation of our Streusel Topping recipe makes a really good, delightful, old-fashioned topping.

2 cups Streusel Topping (next page)
1 cup quick oats
1 cup light brown sugar
1/2 cup chopped walnuts (optional)
1/4 pound (1 stick) butter, cubed

Mix the streusel, oats, and sugar in an upright mixer until well blended. Use the paddle attachment. Be sure you keep the mixer running on low speed or it will start to form a paste. You can add 1/2 cup chopped walnuts (or substitute them for some of the oats) to the crisp topping if you feel a little nutty.

Slowly add cubes of butter, one at a time, until all the butter is incorporated. Mix until it forms marble sized crumbs. This will form a super crisp topping.

To make the crisp, place the fruit filling (next page) in individual ovenproof serving dishes or in an ovenproof pan and spread evenly. Spread the crisp topping over the fruit. It's okay if some of the fruit shows through on the edges. Bake at 350 degrees for 15 minutes and then rotate and bake for 15 more minutes.

Makes 5 cups, or enough for 10 crisps.

Peach & Berry Filling

You can use fresh fruit, but frozen will work great.

4 cups peaches, skins removed
2 cups strawberries or
    1 cup blueberries
2 tablespoons sugar
1 tablespoon cornstarch
1/2 teaspoon dried ginger
1/4 teaspoon ground nutmeg

Combine all ingredients in a mixing bowl. Stir to combine.

Makes enough filling for 5 crisps or a 9–inch pie.

Streusel Topping

We use this to top our fruit pies. This is also the base recipe for the Crisp Topping. The entire staff gathers around and eats this when we make it. I guess that is one of the perks of working in a restaurant.

You can combine these ingredients using a pastry cutter or spoon, but I suggest you save time and use an upright mixer.

1/2 pound (2 sticks) butter, chilled and cubed
1 1/4 cups sugar
2 1/4 cups flour

Combine the butter and sugar in an upright mixer until well blended. Slowly add the flour—slowly, or else you will end up with a big flour cloud all over you and your kitchen. The mixture is done when it forms pea-sized crumbs. That happens relatively quickly, so stay there and watch it while it mixes.

Makes 6 cups, or enough for 4 pies.

The Cookie Dough Egg Roll Story

Three years ago, I was making chocolate chip cookies and had a little dough leftover. Amazingly, my wife Melanie didn't eat it all. Our prep cook was making an egg roll appetizer and, as a joke, I grabbed a wrapper, put some cookie dough in it, rolled it up and fried it. That was all it took. I made some for a special that night and it was a hit. It's funny how a joke turned into a signature dish.

Jump forward a year, when I decided to enter The Taste of Madison—an annual event on Madison's Capitol Square that draws thousands of food-loving people. We decided to serve these egg rolls at our booth. I had never done a festival before, and I had no idea what I was getting into. Better said, I had no idea what I was getting Francisca (or Mrs. Tiki, as I call her) into. She rolled and froze 10,000 egg rolls to prepare for this festival. The task took four months of perseverance, dedication, and consistency. We sold 7,500 that year. The next year we sold 10,000.

So, with great appreciation, I say thank you, Mrs. Tiki, for making the **Chocolate Chip Cookie Dough Egg Rolls** what they are today.

Chocolate Chip Cookie Dough Egg Rolls

The Showstopper, Crowd Pleaser, World Famous, One and Only: Bluephies Original Cookie Dough Egg Roll. Taaaaa daaaaaaaaa!

These little guys are my signature item. We feature them in the Taste of Madison (see story, previous page). We sell more every year.

Tip: This is egg-less cookie dough. If you want to add eggs, omit the water and substitute 2 eggs, but it will make the egg rolls SO rich you will barely be able to finish one.

1/4 pound (1 stick) butter
1/2 cup brown sugar
1/2 cup white sugar
1/8 cup water
1 teaspoon vanilla extract
1 teaspoon salt
1 1/8 cups flour
1/2 cup chocolate chips
24 egg roll wrappers, thawed
1/2 gallon of vegetable oil for frying

Blend the butter and sugars in an upright mixer on low speed until it is light and fluffy. Add the water, vanilla, and salt; mix until well blended. Add the flour a little at a time. (If you add it all at once, you'll spend the next half-hour cleaning up the flour dust.) Blend the flour in completely. Finally, add the chocolate chips and just mix to combine.

See our diagram for how to roll these little morsels (page 132). Be sure to freeze them before you fry them—that way they'll hold together.

Heat vegetable oil to 350 degrees in a stockpot or large saucepan. Drop the egg rolls in gently, and fry them in batches for about 2 minutes. Remove from the oil and drain on paper towels.

Makes 24 egg rolls.

(Left) Chocolate Chip Cookie Dough Egg Rolls *served with vanilla ice cream and drizzled with chocolate sauce*

How to Make an Egg Roll

1. Put a scoop of filling near one corner of the egg roll wrap.

2. Flatten the dough a bit and fold 1/3 of the wrap over it.

3. Roll the egg roll toward the middle.

4. Moisten with a bit of water and fold one side toward middle.

5. Fold other side toward middle to make an envelope.

6. Finish rolling (continued next page).

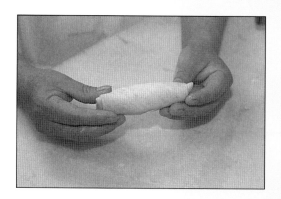

7. Moisten end-flap with a small amount of water, and seal egg roll.

"Thank you, Mrs. Tiki, for making the **Chocolate Chip Cookie Dough Egg Rolls** what they are today."

Back in the Days

I got my start in the restaurant business at my mom's place, working as a busboy. I really wanted to cook but, in Chicago, you have to be eighteen. I was sixteen when we moved to Madison and I got a job working the breakfast shift at an east side restaurant. That's how I learned to cook fast. If you didn't have moves and work fast, you got canned.

I started working lunches and dinner there, but it wasn't fun. I was just flinging burgers and sandwiches. There was no challenge; everyone there was just working for a paycheck. I wanted to learn more, so I looked for another job. I went to a local steak house one night for dinner and thought that I could do what they did. I went up to the bar and asked the owner for an application. I waited about a week and nothing happened. Then Mother's Day came, their dishwasher quit, and they called me. I raced over and found mountains of dirty dishes, pans, silverware, and glasses. I jumped right in. I finally finished and got to eat at about eleven that night. I stayed. I liked working there; it was a challenge.

Soon the kitchen manager—a real taskmaster—said he'd hire me as the prep-cook if I washed all the dishes, too. I did, and I can still wash dishes faster than anyone. I ended up as their fry cook. This place was so busy that for Friday fish fry they had three fryers going. I also had to fry the hash browns. Every Friday we cooked 500 pounds of cod and 1000 pounds of potatoes.

When the chef couldn't take the stress and walked out, the owner was stuck between a rock and a hard place. I stayed, so at age seventeen, I got to work as the lead line cook.

I started college planning to be a social worker. I discovered that it was the wrong choice for me because I like things orderly and predictable. All that time, I kept working as a short-order cook. Soon after I dropped out of college, I got a job with a chef who showed me how incredible cooking could be. Craig opened up new worlds for me and then encouraged me to get more education and work other places with different people.

At 20, I had worked for four great cooks, and I had been an assistant to the chef instructor at the Madison Area Technical College. I was determined to succeed, I worked very hard and I landed my first chef job. Then, out of the blue, Craig called, "You want to be my chef?" Two weeks later, I moved. It was the coolest job I had ever had. I loved it. I got to do what I wanted and made a living doing it. **I was hooked.**

Billy Horzuesky makes recipes
your mom never made you.

INDEX